MW00534197

"*Leading Faithful Innovation: Following God into a Hopeful Future* is a must-read for congregational leaders today. The authors not only make the case for faithful innovation and experimentation in congregational ministry but outline how to actually put it into practice. This is not a handbook on the latest gimmicks for church growth but, rather, a model for church life where leaders intentionally listen to God's voice (starting with Scripture), act on what is heard, and then share subsequent learnings with others. Along the way, leaders may find their own lives transformed as their congregations become centers for faithful innovation in Christ's name."

—Rev. Tracie L. Bartholomew, bishop of
the New Jersey Synod, ELCA

"For too long the church has mistaken the ideology of progress for the hope of new creation. Moreover, we have blindly accepted the corporate world's fascination with creative destruction while sacrificing true Christian innovation. This has led to devastating consequences for congregations and communities. *Leading Faithful Innovation* invites us to embark on a journey of new creation that draws us into the very triune life of God. Introducing us to simple prayerful practices that help us discern and join what God is up to in our daily lives, this book opens up revolutionary pathways for new expressions of healing, community, and faith to flourish in the world."

—Michael Adam Beck, pastor, professor, author, director
of Fresh Expressions US, director of Fresh Expressions
House of Studies at United Theological Seminary

"This book is designed specifically for congregations who want to find new ways to live out the old faith. It is for Christian leaders who desire faithful innovation."

—Scott Cormode, Hugh De Pree Professor of Leadership Development, Fuller Seminary

"If you are struggling to experience and name the power of the living God in your midst, this book is for you. *Leading Faithful Innovation* will help you listen for God, identify hope, and take risks in love. You will be given a viable path—*a way of life*—for creating new practices in your community. The kind of innovation this encouraging book invites will cultivate Christian faith in ways that will substantially impact people's identity and daily life—yours and others'."

—Angela Williams Gorrell, author of *The Gravity of Joy: A Story of Being Lost and Found*

"A timely book filled with helpful wisdom and insight that pushes beyond an overly simplistic programmatic approach toward a full embrace of our deeper call as the church to be a Spirit-led, outward-focused, relationship-based, community-building movement for a rapidly changed and still changing, post-pandemic world. It's time for the church to learn how to let go and follow—rather than attempt to control and lead—God."

—Mike Housholder, senior pastor, Lutheran Church of Hope, West Des Moines, Iowa

"Provocative and inspiring in equal measure, *Leading Faithful Innovation* will kindle your thinking about how God is inviting us to live as a church in new ways. Anyone and everyone who cares about being a more effective Christian disciple will cherish this book. And it is a remarkable textbook with lessons for leadership in any sector."

—Linda Koch Lorimer, vice president for international and strategic initiatives, emerita, Yale University

"Rarely do authors present such a comprehensive work that accomplishes both the elegance of rooted theology and the depth of experience of decades of practice. *Leading Faithful Innovation* is an essential tool for denominational leaders, pastors, and people of the church who are not content with the current status quo and want to join God in creating a better future for the world."

—Nicholas Warnes, executive director of Cyclical, Inc.; author of *Starting Missional Churches* and *Deconstructing Church Planting*

# leading faithful
# INNOVATION

Following
God into a
**Hopeful
Future**

leading faithful
INNOVATION

Dwight Zscheile
Michael Binder
Tessa Pinkstaff

Fortress Press
Minneapolis

LEADING FAITHFUL INNOVATION
Following God into a Hopeful Future

Cover design and illustration: Kristin Miller

Print ISBN: 978-1-5064-8876-9
eBook ISBN: 978-1-5064-8877-6

# Contents

# Acknowledgments

The learning shared in this book is the result of many years of working with congregations alongside numerous collaborators. We have benefited greatly from the contributions of several colleagues whose works provided a foundation upon which we built, refined, and articulated the frameworks found in our chapters. Our former Luther Seminary colleagues Craig Van Gelder, Patrick Keifert, and Gary Simpson shaped much of how we think about God's mission, the church, culture, and congregational change. Alan Roxburgh and Fiona Watts from The Missional Network (TMN) pioneered earlier versions of the faithful innovation journey, bringing together innovation theory and congregational revitalization. Mark Lau Branson's work on the topics of Appreciative Inquiry, listening carefully to stories and framing leadership as an invitation into God's mission, has also influenced us deeply, as has Scott Cormode's writing on Christian innovation.

Our colleagues from Luther Seminary's Faith+Lead team have been significant learning partners on this journey. We're especially grateful to Dawn Alitz, Jon Anderson, Terri Elton, Alicia Granholm, Rolf Jacobson, Katie Langston, Grace Pomroy, and Dee Stokes for their thoughtful contributions to the work of faithful innovation and to this book specifically. The entire Faith+Lead team has been an inspiration to us as we've collaborated on helping the church address the challenge of forming Christian community in contemporary cultures.

We have had the privilege to work with hundreds of congregations and denominational systems over the past decade or more. It is through journeying with these partners that we have learned to conceptualize the faithful innovation process the way we do in this book. Without them, this book would not exist. We have included many of their stories in the chapters that follow, and while the lessons we learned are real, we have changed details or withheld information out of respect for our participants' privacy. We are profoundly grateful to all the people who have been willing to listen carefully, try new things, and learn from the process.

Part of this work was made possible by the Lilly Endowment, Inc. They generously funded Luther Seminary's Leadership for Faithful Innovation grant, which allowed us to walk with nearly fifty congregations in six Evangelical Lutheran Church in America (ELCA) synods over a four-year period.

A range of colleagues in the wider church and academy took the time to read and respond to drafts of this book, including Kathy Brekken, Scott Cormode, David Hayes, Tim Hodapp, Gary Johnson, Trevor Kaihoi, Harvey Kwiyani, Terese Lewis, Heidi Macias, Mac McCarthy, and Bill Withers. Their careful attention to the manuscript helped us clarify and hone our argument.

Finally, we are grateful for our readers because you, like us, are curious about discovering a new way to be the church in the twenty-first century. We thank God for the calling on your life and for the ministry contexts in which you serve. We humbly pray that this book might be a catalyst for spiritual transformation in your community.

# Introduction

## Defining Faithful Innovation

The church that James had been a member of for decades was aging and struggling. He and other faithful members were well past retirement and didn't have the same energy they once did to serve on committees and volunteer for programs. No matter how attractive they tried to make the congregation, younger people in the neighborhood didn't seem interested in attending or joining. Most poignantly, very few of their own children or grandchildren had anything to do with church. His own daughter was committed to living a good life, but she had little time for church, and her children were being raised without a meaningful Christian faith.[1]

---

Ellen was a board member at a growing nondenominational church in a suburban area that was successfully attracting families from a similar cultural and social demographic. They had tailored the church experience to speak to this audience, from the music and worship to the children's and youth ministries and small groups. However, their suburb was rapidly changing, with newer immigrant neighbors moving in. The church didn't know how to connect with these neighbors across differences of race and culture, to say nothing of neighbors in nearby areas across differences of class.

———————————

Deborah was pastor of a midsized congregation that had survived the pandemic mostly intact but not without cost. Her leadership team had moved the congregation's worship and activities online as best they could, and most members remained connected. Yet Deborah and the other leaders were worn out. Even before the pandemic, she had struggled to keep the "machine" of the congregation's activities and programs running. Doing it while negotiating conflicting pandemic health and safety expectations and trying to keep everything and everyone together brought Deborah to the brink of utter exhaustion. She was thinking seriously about leaving the ministry. At the same time, Deborah had discovered a group of amazing women through her neighborhood yoga studio. They would sometimes linger after class to share stories, and many were opening up about their spiritual struggles. None of them were part of a church, and Deborah realized there was little in the congregation she served that would make sense to them. Deborah was caught between wanting to go deeper in relationship with these women and physically having to pull herself away from conversations with them to get back to managing the church.

———————————

You're reading this book because you're facing changes that aren't easy to navigate. Many established ways of doing church are breaking down, and you aren't sure how to respond. Perhaps you're worn out from trying to sustain an old model of church, and you're not sure what the alternative is. Fewer people are willing to join, serve, volunteer in, and support congregations in today's cultures. People in the neighborhood are seeking spiritual meaning and purpose, but little in your church's present life may be designed to connect with their longings and losses—the worries, fears, and dreams that keep them up at night.[2]

You may find yourself doing church in a hybrid mode, where you're reaching people online but don't know how to deepen connections with them. Or maybe you know you need to embrace digital ways of doing ministry, but you don't know what this would mean for being a Christian community. For many of us, things that used to work in previous seasons of ministry no longer work, and there are no clear answers about what the future holds.

We've been there too. The three of us have worked with churches of many kinds whose leaders (lay and ordained, at all levels) are experiencing the kind of loss and disorientation that you might be going through. We've seen firsthand some key things that work and those that don't, why some churches thrive and others do not. We've learned some vital lessons that we will share over the course of this book.

We've also recently lived through a time when change was forced upon all of us. Much of it was the kind of change that takes things away and leaves loss in its wake. The pandemic disrupted settled patterns in the church and society, accelerating trends of institutional disaffiliation and disengagement while also surfacing divisions and injustices. Accelerating change seems to be the norm in a world where technological and social transformations are constantly speeding up. It's easy to feel like the ground under our feet is perpetually shifting.

Yet change also opens hopeful possibilities for life together. As we navigate new ways of being the church, we don't want to lose what is precious and transcendent. For Christians, this is the good news of God's love for the world in Jesus. The power of God's promises anchors us even amid tumultuous seas. We yearn to stay rooted and connected in God's love—to abide in the true vine (John 15:1–11)—when so much seems in flux. In a world of constant innovation, how can we stay focused and true to our callings and offer a countercultural witness?

This is the work of *faithful innovation*—learning new ways to embody Christian identity and purpose in a changing context. It includes listening to God, one another, and our neighbors; trying experiments that lead us into new ways of thinking; and reflecting on what we've learned as we tell stories about God's movement in our congregations and communities. It's about adopting practices and habits that allow the treasures of the Christian faith to speak afresh today. Often, it involves the rediscovery of ancient spiritual practices as much as the discovery of new technologies. Faithful innovation is an invitation to deepen connections. It is a way to simplify, refocus, and reorient ourselves and our communities. It is an opportunity to become less busy, less distracted, and more open to God's leading. It is not another program, to-do list, or thing to add on top of already busy schedules. Rather, it is a way of life, a journey of discovery that draws us back into core stories of the faith and deepens our capacity to be led by God.

Faithful innovation is the process of learning new ways to embody Christian identity and purpose in a changing cultural context. It is about rediscovering how to be the church in the twenty-first century and reconnecting with God, one another, and neighbors.

## An Unexpected Journey

[Paul and his companions] went through the region of Phrygia and Galatia, having been forbidden by the Holy Spirit to speak the word in Asia. When they had come opposite Mysia, they attempted to go into Bithynia, but the Spirit of Jesus did not allow them; so, passing by Mysia, they went down to Troas. During the night Paul had a vision: there stood a man of Macedonia pleading with him and saying, "Come over to Macedonia and help us." When he had seen the vision, we immediately tried to cross over to Macedonia, being convinced that God had called us to proclaim the good news to them. We therefore set sail from Troas and took a straight course to Samothrace, the following day to Neapolis, and from there to Philippi, which is a leading city of the district of Macedonia and a Roman colony. We remained in this city for some days. On the Sabbath day we went outside the gate by the river, where we supposed there was a place of prayer, and we sat down and spoke to the women who had gathered there. A certain woman named Lydia, a worshiper of God, was listening to us; she was from the city of Thyatira and a dealer in purple cloth. The Lord opened her heart to listen eagerly to what was said by Paul. When she and her household were baptized, she urged us, saying, "If you have judged me to be faithful to the Lord, come and stay at my home." And she prevailed upon us. (Acts 16:6–15)

This story from Acts embodies the key themes of this book. Jesus's followers are led by the Holy Spirit on a path where the destination isn't clear when they start. The road isn't straightforward. They discover where to go by listening, acting, and reflecting. They must practice being hosted by others in neighborhood spaces they don't control. They are redirected multiple times as dead ends lead to open doors but not necessarily the open doors they expected. Throughout, they must depend on God's leading, not their own strategies and plans.

This is the kind of journey that characterizes much of what we read in the New Testament about the early church. The Jesus movement was about a group of strangers and friends being joined together by God into a community practicing a distinct way of life that crossed cultural and geographical boundaries. That movement was animated by the life-giving, loving energy of the Holy Spirit, which broke down walls, bound people together, and freed them to take risks in love. It was a subversive movement that called into question the predominant stories and structures of the day.

> Following the Holy Spirit means we might not know where we're going, but we must make a move to discover the next step. We must trust our ability to sense God's leading. We might be surprised by what God has in store for us.

Many church leaders today find themselves on an unexpected journey. Many of us were taught to follow the twentieth-century blueprints of modern managerial change, where we could confidently identify an organizational destination and manage people into it. But these ancient biblical stories of discernment and improvisation are far more helpful today. Rather than assume it is all up to us to create a successful organizational future through our own energy, planning, and technique, we must relearn how to be led by God's Spirit like the early apostles, exercising both patience and the willingness to move quickly and responsively.

This is a very different kind of journey, with a very different mindset. For those of us in Western cultures conditioned to seek the good without God, it may be difficult to recognize God's presence, power, and agency. This journey means learning to pay attention to the Holy Spirit in new ways. For those in global majority cultures and communities of color that are not as secularized as the West, it means leaning into God's leading while facing the ambiguity and complexity of a challenging social and cultural environment. No context today is immune from change, and with that change comes opportunity as well as loss. So what does faithfulness look like in such a time?

## Learning to Ask God Questions

In our work with congregations, we usually hear what Alan Roxburgh calls "church questions."[3] These are questions like, *How can we get more people to join our church? How can our church meet a need in the neighborhood? How can we attract more young families?* These questions are understandable, arising from genuine concern for the church and for our neighbors. However, they tend to default toward a posture of fixing the church. Our focus becomes centered on what *we* can do to sustain or grow the church as an institution. God's role tends to drop out of view.

Moreover, our neighbors can easily become abstractions ("young families," "the needy") rather than actual people with whom we have relationships and whose stories we know. We can turn them into objects of attraction or fixing according to our visions and plans for them. We can lose sight of their needs, desires, feelings, will, and power—their agency as subjects in their own right, people among whom God is already at work.

This book invites ministry leaders to change the questions their communities ask from "church questions" to "God questions."[4] God questions can't be answered through strategic plans and managerial solutions. They require a different posture of listening, discernment (paying attention to God), experimentation, and reflection in community. They draw us closer to God and our neighbors—not as objects but as particular people like Lydia in Acts 16, with unique stories, yearnings, and dreams. They may be asking questions like, *Why is there evil? How can humans find deeper purpose in the world? Where can I find hope? How can I be unified with people with whom I differ and disagree?*

"God questions" ask, *What might God be up to in the lives of our neighbors? Where has God been present in the history of our congregation? How might the Spirit be moving in the lives of our church's members or calling us to join God's work in the neighborhood?*

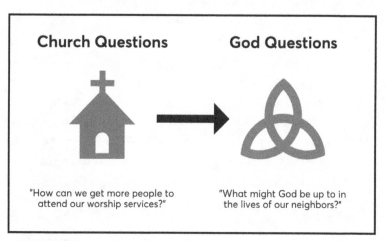

## Church Questions → God Questions

"How can we get more people to attend our worship services?"

"What might God be up to in the lives of our neighbors?"

See Alan J. Roxburgh, *Joining God, Remaking Church, Changing the World* (New York: Morehouse, 2015), ix.

We believe that the church's future is waiting to be discovered not inside the walls of church buildings or in committee meetings but on journeys into the neighborhood, "outside the gate" at the "place of prayer" (Acts 16:13) where the spiritually curious gather in dynamic relationship with both the Spirit of God and the Lydias of our own day. The social and cultural shifts that are eroding established church structures are too big for any of us to reverse. Trying to "fix" the church will not get us very far and will instead distract us from the deeper work at hand. We need a very different kind of imagination, approach, and set of practices.

## Why Church?

Acts 16 can seem like a strange text to readers today. These early followers of Jesus were so passionate about sharing the healing, redemption, and reconciliation they had experienced in Christ that they were willing to undertake arduous and ambiguous journeys so that others might know that power firsthand. They were compelled to share with others their own stories of Jesus. Many churchgoers today would be hard-pressed to articulate a message that would drive them to make such a personal sacrifice. Indeed, they may struggle to name the difference Jesus makes in their own lives. When people are unable to explain their faith in the relatively safe confines of conversations with family and fellow congregants, sharing the hope of Jesus with neighbors and strangers can seem even more daunting.

The apostles in Acts 16 took that risky journey because of the transformation they experienced in Christ. When they met Lydia and entered into conversation with her, they assumed she was looking for something her present life and spiritual quest had not provided. That was why she was outside the gates at this place of prayer on the Sabbath, why she was baptized, and why she took the risk of inviting these Jewish men to stay with her in her home. Something life changing is at stake here in this encounter. It plays out through mutual invitation, with the giving and receiving of stories, and through hospitality, which in this case happened across cultural lines.

All of this leads to some challenging questions. *What is life changing at the heart of your Christian faith and in your church? What difference does Jesus make to you personally, to the life of your church, and to our world? Who are the Lydias in your life and your context, and what are they struggling with and looking for? How might the gospel of Jesus speak to those longings and losses?* These are questions that you might not be able to answer easily. Perhaps little in your experience of church has focused on answering them.

Yet unless we can discover some clarity around the answers, we won't be able to address a core underlying question: *Why Jesus?* What distinctive contribution does the gospel of Jesus make to people's lives? The related question is, *Why church?* As the bearer of God's redemptive mission for the world, the church offers real, transformative hope for humankind through Jesus. But if the church isn't making a noticeable difference in how people think, live, and engage with their communities, no wonder people are disengaging, disinterested, or even deeply skeptical about it.

We believe the best way to answer these questions is not to focus on trying to fix the church but to focus on God and the everyday lives of our neighbors—the Lydias in our contexts. The journey of faithful innovation is about simple practices of listening to God, one another, and our neighbors and engaging in simple experiments of being present in the spaces of our wider communities where life takes place. Through these practices, we begin to identify how God might be leading us into deeper relationships, connections, and community and where the gospel story speaks in conversation with the stories of our neighbors.

## Why "Faithful"?

We use the term "faithful" in this book to signify several things. First, the kind of innovation we're describing is Spirit led. We believe that the triune God is active in the world today. The Holy Spirit is the primary leader of the church, and the role of human leaders is to help the community listen to and be led by God. Faithfulness is about recognizing, attending to, and participating in the triune God's leadership. Secular theories and tools—some of which we will draw on in this book—can be very helpful, but only within a larger theological framework that prioritizes divine presence and agency.

> " The Holy Spirit is the primary leader of the church, and the role of human leaders is to help the community listen to and be led by God. "

This is important because many of the churches we've worked with over the years have an underlying challenge: they struggle to form Christian identity, practice, and community with their own members, their children, and their neighbors. Whatever organizational challenges they're facing are secondary to the root issue of not knowing how to cultivate Christian discipleship in contemporary culture. This was less of a problem historically when the surrounding culture broadly supported Christian affiliation and participation. At that time, it could be assumed that Christian practices and the

Christian story were instilled in the home. But that is not the case today—at least for the vast majority. So many of today's churches in Western cultures are simply not focused on or designed to cultivate disciples.

"Faithful" in this sense means cultivating Christian faith in ways that are consequential to human identity and daily life. As noted above, many churches are struggling and failing because they have not cast a clear vision for the difference Jesus makes in daily life or formed people in the practices by which that vision comes to life among the whole people of God. Faithful discipleship in today's world isn't about going along with the narratives, assumptions, and norms of the broader culture, which have diverged profoundly from Christian teachings. It means instead cultivating a countercultural way of life. Because of the radical call of Jesus, Christian people are supposed to live differently, and the church is supposed to help them do that. But when churches fail to help people live into a distinctive Christian identity and way of life, they will continue to struggle and, tragically, even cease to exist.

So discovering and rediscovering faithfulness to God's leadership and God's promises are central to the work many churches need to do today. This involves cultivating practices by which people can experience the power and presence of God for themselves and, in turn, reflect on their experience in community. The journey we're inviting you on is about encountering the God who created the world, freed Israel from bondage in Egypt, raised Jesus from the dead, and promised to be with us until the end of time. Experiences of that God—and the stories we share about those divine encounters—should be at the center of the church's life. It is the Holy Spirit's energy—not our own—that animates the life of the church. Faithfulness means attending to the triune God's presence, promises, and movement, even and especially amid ordinary encounters in daily life.

> " The journey we're inviting you on is about encountering the God who created the world, freed Israel from bondage in Egypt, raised Jesus from the dead, and promised to be with us until the end of time. "

## What Do We Mean by "Innovation"?

The term "innovation" is used in today's world to mean different things. People often associate it with *invention*—starting from scratch to create something new. For churches, this sounds both intimidating (*Isn't invention for those rare geniuses?*) and unsettling (*We will have to abandon our precious traditions!*). Faced with this understanding of innovation, no wonder people are inclined to turn away, double down on current practices, and resist change.

"Innovation" can also evoke a late-modern Silicon Valley culture of uninhibited disruption of institutions and cultural norms through technology—the "move fast and break things" mantra of Big Tech. We've seen how this kind of innovation has undercut democracy; fostered alienation, anxiety, and depression; divided the populace; and led to massive economic displacement for many, even as it has generated extraordinary wealth for some.

Underneath these understandings of innovation is the assumption that the new is always better than the old, everything must constantly change, and if we don't join the juggernaut of technological "progress," we will be run over by it. There is a utopianism in this understanding of technology that assumes we can perfect humanity with the right tools. It runs roughshod over human history, human traditions, and human communities. The hamster wheel of this kind of technological innovation speeds faster and faster, leaving many of us behind. If this is what "innovation" means, we should rightly be suspicious of it and even resist it in the name of faithfulness to the gospel.

When we use the word "innovation" in this book, we don't mean any of these things. We have a much simpler definition: *the adoption of a new practice in a community*.[5] In the case of innovation in the church, it is often an ancient practice that needs to be rediscovered. As Scott Cormode asks, "How do we maintain a rock-solid commitment to the unchanging Christian faith while at the same time finding innovative ways to express that faith in an ever-changing culture?"[6] We want to be clear that for us, innovation is not invention. It does not start from scratch or reject tradition wholesale. Rather, it is the adaptation of Christian community life and witness to changing cultural circumstances. This is what the church has always done—from the beginning until now, across countless diverse cultural contexts around the world and throughout history.

It is also decidedly not about jumping on a hamster wheel of frantic activity and technical solutions to try to be "relevant" in a culture skeptical of the church. We see many leaders and congregations burning out trying to find the right activity, program, or quick fix that will turn around the trends of institutional decline. A congregation calls on their leader in the hope that the leader's energy will animate and catalyze a new surge of members (especially young ones!), volunteers, and resources. This is an understandable desire but fundamentally misdirected.

The kind of innovation we will explore in this book moves in a very different direction. It is about identifying and introducing simple, life-giving practices rooted in ancient traditions of the church that help people connect more deeply with God, one another, and their neighbors. These practices are innovative insofar as they are new within the life of the congregation and involve new learning. Sometimes they are reformulations of ancient practices in more accessible forms. They are rooted deeply in Christian wisdom and tradition and fruitfully subvert contemporary cultural norms. For instance, learning to listen patiently and deeply is a profoundly countercultural practice in today's society of social media and cultural tribalism. Such empathetic listening that builds bridges across cultural and political differences can be a sign of reconciliation and hope—an alternative path to what society offers.

Above all, innovation as we explore it in this book recognizes the agency and activity of God as the ultimate innovator. God continues to create, re-create, restore, reconcile, and heal the world. The Scriptures repeatedly attest to God doing a new thing (Isa 43:19; 2 Cor 5:17). As we take the faithful innovation journey, our hope is not in the latest technology or our own wisdom but in the power of God, who promises to make all things new and who is at work in the most seemingly godforsaken places in the world. The Spirit of God is at work among the whole people of God, at the grassroots, renewing and making whole, guiding and directing. Faithful innovation is about joining the Spirit's movement.

## What Do We Mean by "Leadership"?

This is a book about leadership, which is another highly contested term. There are many cultural models of leadership functioning in the church today, some more helpful and faithful to the gospel than others. At its most basic level, leadership is simply a process of relational influence.[7] When we use the term "leadership," we also have a specific paradigm in mind. The primary leader of the church is God through the Holy Spirit. Faithful innovation is about learning to be influenced by God in order to join in what God is doing in the world. Faithful innovation requires ordering a Christian community's life so that people can attend to and discover the Spirit's leading, not only corporately but also personally in their daily lives.

What does this mean for human leadership? It is not up to human leaders to bring an exciting vision, sell it to the congregation, and try to compel people to enact it to reach a destination the leader has predetermined. Rather, if the Spirit of God is alive among the people of God—which we firmly believe—then the task for human leaders is to create the conditions under which the people can deepen their attentiveness to God's influence in their lives. Faithfully innovative leadership is less about managing what is truly God's work and more about cultivating an environment in which God acts. Leaders actively plant and water the seeds while God is responsible for the growth (1 Cor 3:6).[8] This happens through simple, accessible practices—many of which we will discuss in this book.

> " It is not up to human leaders to bring an exciting vision, sell it to the congregation, and try to compel people into enacting it to reach a destination the leader has predetermined. "

Often, the direction of God's leadership is not easy to determine ahead of time. It doesn't fit easily into five-year strategic plans. Biblically, as we saw in Acts 16, it more commonly unfolds through experiences of encounters with neighbors, conversations among believers, life-giving connections, and trial and error. It is not linear. The inherent ambiguity in discerning God's leading (and the real risk we can get it wrong) pushes us deeper into Scripture, deeper into prayer, deeper into reflection in community (especially across cultural differences), and deeper into experimentation. We learn as we go. There is no end to discerning; it must be continuous. We approach it with a posture of humility and curiosity, ready to pivot and change direction as the Holy Spirit directs us.

Leading faithful innovation means cultivating a community of listening on multiple levels inside and outside of the church, of prayer and spiritual practices, and of action learning, whereby people behave their way forward into a new future rather than plan everything out ahead of time. It means lovingly holding space in a community for people's yearnings, fears, anxieties, and hopes, recognizing that your role as a leader is not to fix people, rescue them from the ambiguities they're facing, or tell them where to go. Rather, it means introducing the practices by which people can discover a hopeful future and do the learning themselves while you walk alongside them, helping them interpret faithfully what they are experiencing. In this model, leadership, or influence, comes primarily *from* God and is worked out *through* the people of God. Human leaders are cultivators, midwives, communal storytellers, and architects of community life and practice.

## The Faithful Innovation Journey

We invite you on a journey of discovery. In chapter 1, we will examine some of the conditions churches find themselves in as we've entered the early twenty-first century. This is a time both of profound disruption and of great opportunity and promise. We'll seek to provide more context for why many established structures are failing as well as why this is also a great time to be the church. We'll do so by paying more attention to Lydia, who represents the spiritually curious but institutionally disconnected people in today's world.

From there, in chapters 2–4, we'll delve into the three core practices of faithful innovation: Listen, Act, and Share. These practices provide the way forward for churches facing any number of challenges for which there are no easy answers. We'll share stories of Christian communities that have been on this journey and include details on how this work is embodied concretely in congregational life.

| Listen | → | Act | → | Share |
|---|---|---|---|---|
| Listen to God, one another, and our neighbors. | | Try something new based on God's leading. | | Reflect on your actions and share your story. |

Chapters 5 and 6 step back to reflect on how congregational life can be reshaped in order to support faithful innovation and what leadership looks like in more detail. What we're offering is not a technique or program but rather a way of life for churches. It is not a to-do list or another add-on for pastors who are already overburdened. What we're advocating is a way of life that puts God back in the center. We'll explore more about what's at stake in that and how congregations and their leaders can discover new hope, energy, and vitality. Finally, we'll revisit the question of where churches can discover hope amid the changes and challenges of today.

The ideas in this book come from our own trial-and-error experiences leading and accompanying hundreds of congregations over a decade in a variety of contexts around the United States. In our work on Luther Seminary's Faith+Lead team, as well as our own experiences as pastors and consultants, we have been blessed to work with a range of congregations struggling to address challenges for which there are no easy answers. Our process has been developed and refined in collaboration with them. We are indebted to those we've served, as they've shaped our learning through their own successes and failures. The learning process is ongoing. We continue to be learners ourselves, and the journey we invite you into is open-ended.

# One

## Why Lydia Doesn't Go to Your Church

Yolanda came home from work to an empty house, and the familiar loneliness settled in. Though successful professionally, Yolanda felt a sense of hollowness about all the energy she was spending to survive at work in a cutthroat corporate environment. It seemed like a futile race to run, but she was terrified to face what might happen if she stepped off that treadmill. Yolanda was painfully aware of the disconnect between the injustice she saw and experienced in the world and her ability to do much about it. She picked up her iPad and started scrolling through Instagram and Facebook, which just made her feel worse. Yolanda was looking forward to going for a hike over the weekend—maybe she would feel some peace in nature. But a nagging unease lingered.

---

Gordon glanced up from his video game; it was past midnight. The hours had flown by, and he felt the sickening feeling of having little to show for them. Gordon and his friends—all in their early twenties—didn't know where they belonged in an economy and a culture that seemed to have forgotten people in small towns like his, especially those who didn't go to college. Though he had tried drugs like so many of his peers, he had abandoned them soon afterward, having seen too much firsthand evidence of where that led. So many of his parents' milestones seemed like distant dreams, from marriage and starting a family to having a place of his own. Gordon's grandmother tried to get him to go to church, but he had to work Sundays. Besides, he thought, the people at church would just judge him, like they judged everyone else. He wondered, *Is this all there is?*

You know Lydia. In your family, your circle of friends, your workplace, and your neighborhood, there are people everywhere who are disconnected from organized religion but who are still seeking spiritual meaning, purpose, and community. The biblical Lydia of Acts 16 was a gentile (a non-Jew) from the city of Thyatira who was living in Philippi, a Macedonian town where Paul and his companions encountered her. She was a dealer in purple cloth, which would have been a luxury good at the time, and ran her own household. This suggests that she was a prosperous, independent businesswoman. Acts 16 describes her as a "worshiper of God" (v. 14)—someone whose spiritual curiosity and openness had led her to the place of prayer outside the city gates where Paul and the others found her. Her spiritual search had taken her beyond the city and its temples and institutions.

In today's world, and particularly in Western societies, increasing numbers of people are pursuing their spiritual journeys outside the walls of churches, synagogues, mosques, or other religious institutions. The vast majority of these people are not atheists (in the United States, for instance, only 4 percent of the population identifies as atheists and 5 percent as agnostics[1]). Yet the religiously unaffiliated—the so-called nones—are now almost a third of the American population. This vast category is largely composed of people who are detached from religion but who are not actively opposed to faith. Their longings and losses could be addressed by what faith in Jesus offers.

It's also important to keep in mind that many people who consider themselves Christian (and identify as such on religious affiliation surveys) find themselves outside of the institutional church too. Many can't find a congregation to join where they feel they belong or can engage meaningfully. Of those who attend church only a few times each year, nearly 40 percent say they don't go more often because they practice their faith in other ways.[2] Religious faith is increasingly moving outside the walls of the church. Because the church was intended to be the center of discipleship, there is a growing concern about the kind of Christianity that is developing without the guidance of the larger church community.

The Lydias of our world are these kinds of spiritual seekers who are often located outside of traditional church structures. We inhabit a cultural moment where people of faith have many spiritual options and significantly less social pressure to join a religious organization. In fact, this is a time when institutions of all sorts are coming under withering critique, and religious institutions are no exception. While the cultural conditions in America and other Western societies in previous generations generally favored Christianity and specifically favored participating in a congregation, those days are either long gone or quickly fading (depending on your particular context). This chapter will explore some of the cultural and social changes that are affecting churches and other institutions, making it increasingly unlikely that today's Lydias will come to your church. We'll also reflect together on how God's promises in Jesus can be a matter of life or death for those very neighbors and how reclaiming those promises can reinvigorate existing Christian communities.

## The Age of Association

Let's begin with a quick look back in history. In the US context, we are inheritors of a whole paradigm of institutional church that is increasingly at odds with contemporary culture. (Readers in other global contexts may find this description resonates to a greater or lesser extent with their specific histories and realities.) There are massive changes taking place in the basic way in which the American church is organized, funded, supported, and engaged, and we must recognize them for what they are.

Prior to the American Revolution, the church in the American colonies carried over a basic blueprint from the European state churches, with some important modifications. Church and state in early America were deeply interwoven in a geographical parish system. Many people weren't as active in church as we often imagine them to be, and in some places (such as Puritan New England), membership was restricted to a particular group and often excluded outsiders. In other places, church attendance was more a function of being born in a particular place (and baptized and registered in the local parish). The church took responsibility for social functions like public education, and the state exercised governance over the church. What was different in America compared to Europe was the overlapping of these systems of geographical religious domains as greater religious tolerance became the norm. In other words, different kinds of Christians lived in close proximity in a specific area.

After the Revolution, this system was legally and formally disestablished with the separation of church and state, and a new paradigm emerged. Ted Smith calls this the "Age of Association."[3] In this model, the church became what was known as a "voluntary association," which members could choose to affiliate with, join, and support through contributions (rather than government taxes). Freed from state control, churches could organize and govern themselves and compete in a religious marketplace for members and support.

The church was not the only institution that embraced the Age of Association. All kinds of organizations, from the Freemasons to Rotary Clubs, emerged in this period as a means by which people came together to accomplish some purpose. French diplomat Alexis de Tocqueville, a keen observer of American politics, famously described these voluntary associations in his two-volume book *Democracy in America* (published in 1835 and 1840), noting the dynamism and vitality they brought to American society. The system of American representative democracy emerged in this period, as did countless other community, cultural, social, and service organizations. Denominations, understood as one legitimate religious option within a pluralistic environment, are a product of this period. Denominations were formed around ethnic and doctrinal identities to connect congregations for governance, resource sharing, and organizing for domestic and foreign missions.

These voluntary associations were often restrictive, with women and racial minorities in particular excluded from participation and/or leadership. Women and minorities started their own voluntary organizations as they struggled with marginalization in mainstream institutions. Women's aid societies or Black denominations would be examples. The overall paradigm assumed a strong degree of institutional trust and commitment and a willingness to join and sacrificially serve these organizations. Many of the older members in today's congregations grew up under this system. For these elders, this basic paradigm still works, providing meaningful connection, engagement, and purpose.

## The Age of Authenticity

However, beginning in the late 1960s, the culture began to shift from the Age of Association to what the philosopher Charles Taylor calls the "Age of Authenticity."[4] In the Age of Authenticity, the focus is on discovering and expressing one's true self. Identity is understood as something constructed and performed by the individual rather than something ascribed through the person's location among a variety of institutions (such as family, neighborhood, congregation, denomination, marriage, career, corporation, etc.). Individuals choose and revise their identities over the course of their lives. The individual self becomes the primary source of authority.

The Age of Authenticity has brought a deep critique of institutions. Some of this is warranted, as patterns of exclusion, injustice, and oppression fostered by institutions have been allowed to persist for decades. These wrongs are now being publicly recognized alongside calls for greater accountability.

Amid this righting of wrongs, however, is a destabilization across institutions. Many people are increasingly leaving their associations without finding or becoming part of new ones. Affiliating with and joining institutions (including Age of Association voluntary organizations) are less meaningful and compelling within the looser connections of the Age of Authenticity. The Age of Authenticity has brought not only liberation from the constrictions of many inherited structures but also the anxiety and fluidity of having to write one's own story, chart one's own path, create community however one can, and make constant choices about basic aspects of one's identity.

Of course, the promise of utter originality in the Age of Authenticity is oversold, as people end up conforming to all kinds of cultural patterns not of their making. Various cultural, social, and economic forces shape each of us, whether we recognize them or not. Expressing one's true self often actually means adopting a model or style found on social media, marketed to us in advertising, or embodied in people we know. Underneath all the rhetoric of individuality are actually a lot of similarities—thus the power of social media "influencers," who can lead thousands or millions of their "followers" to adopt their practices or products.

Where does this leave the church? Most inherited church structures in America were designed for the Age of Association, not the Age of Authenticity.[5] There is a massive generational disengagement from Age of Association institutions of all sorts—scouting, service organizations, clubs, unions, and so on—as younger people are leaving or never joining in the first place. This is much bigger than the church, and there is little church leaders can do to reverse this cultural shift. Trying to sustain an Age of Association organization in the Age of Authenticity is increasingly difficult. This problem has probably already arrived at your church's doorstep. If you're having trouble securing volunteers for committees or your board, or if you've experienced difficulties in getting people to join your congregation formally and pledge to support it, you are seeing this firsthand. These shifts result in fewer and fewer people showing up to church and participating in activities and programs. All of these scenarios are symptoms of larger cultural headwinds.

We live in a transitional period where the Age of Association and Age of Authenticity overlap. This means our response must be nuanced. We should not simply abandon the faithful elders who have sacrificially supported the Age of Association model of church and for whom it remains meaningful. They deserve the church's love, care, and attention. At the same time, we should not expect the inherited model to be viable in most places going forward or to be the vehicle by which the church reaches neighbors who inhabit the cultural framework of the Age of Authenticity.

To return to our Acts 16 metaphor, Lydia probably isn't looking to join and support a voluntary association today. She is most likely looking for belonging, support, and connection as she tries to live out an authentic spiritual life and make a meaningful difference in addressing the challenges facing the world. In this sense, her drive for "authenticity" is a laudable value that the church should embrace, even as the gospel brings an important critique to the idea that the individual self is the center of reality.

## Seeking the Good without God

The shift from the Age of Association to the Age of Authenticity isn't the only cultural transition facing churches today. Western societies are inheritors of a cultural mindset dating back to the European Enlightenment that tends to eclipse God's presence and agency in how people see and experience the world in daily life. The Enlightenment brought many gifts—such as human rights and modern science—that should be celebrated. At the same time, it normalized a shift to describe the world without reference to God.

The arrival of the separation of church and state led to a distinction between secular and sacred spaces in community life. With this new dichotomy, churches began focusing on how to get people to dedicate more of their time, energy, and resources to the "sacred" activities of church rather than the "secular" activities of work, school, or family life. An example would be the unofficial contest that churches wage with their members and communities over youth sports versus church activities (which is mostly a losing battle for churches). Rather than the whole of life and society being perceived as a holistic, integrated reality where God is present and moving, people feel they can only talk about God within certain spheres of activity or in certain spaces. To transgress this is to break a major cultural taboo. These kinds of underlying assumptions mean faith is relegated to a private opinion instead of being a public truth.

Inhabiting a secular age has also come to mean that belief is made fragile for almost everyone.[6] The existence of doubt itself has a long history within the church—the apostle Thomas is a notable example. Yet in a secular age, doubt is a default posture—a cultural norm that is difficult to escape. Belief in God or transcendent reality is just one viable option among many alternatives, and every path, no matter how far it deviates from orthodox faith, is assumed to be equally valid for living a good life. God is understood to be optional to human flourishing. The new mantra becomes *question everything*. The very premise of a sacred reality beyond the material world is questionable in Western cultures.

The flip side to this, however, is that unbelief is also made fragile. People have experiences of mystery, the profound, or uncanny coincidences that don't fit into their secular belief systems. They are caught up short at the birth of a child, feel overwhelmed by a sense of beauty in nature, or experience the comforting presence of a deceased loved one and have no explanation in their worldview for what has occurred.[7] While the default secular way of seeing and experiencing everyday life assumes the self is insulated from external spiritual forces, sometimes that insulation cracks open and becomes more porous, even if momentarily. This is why so many people are interested in spirituality even if they aren't interested in church as they know it.

In a secularized culture, people are on their own to find fullness and meaning. This has led to an acceleration of time; people are moving at a faster pace, trying to cram as many experiences as they can into their lives.[8] As people sense the flatness of daily experience, they respond with a frenetic pace of activity, seeking to secure resources, standing, and a sense of meaning and purpose through working harder and filling their lives with more experiences. Without the rhythms of sacred time and stable relationships that have characterized most human cultures throughout history, life in the modern world can be profoundly alienating. Keeping ever busier and looking for the latest consumer, technological, or entertainment experience may provide a surface level of satisfaction, but underneath lurks a deeper abyss of despair and loneliness.

## A Spiritual Crisis in the Culture

There is a profound spiritual crisis in American society today. This is reflected in the high rates of anxiety and depression (particularly among young people), the "deaths of despair" through suicide and addiction that have risen among working-class people,[9] the polarization and degradation of public discourse, and the widespread division and estrangement in American life. This crisis has both personal and social dimensions, playing out through injustice and social conflict as well as in individual and familial alienation. While there are multiple causes for these realities, they have arisen in a deep spiritual vacuum in the culture.

> " *There is a profound spiritual crisis in American society today.* "

Many of the institutions and practices that held a diverse society together are under strain to the breaking point or have collapsed entirely. The Covid-19 pandemic isolated an already lonely populace that no longer found support in many of the traditional structures of community life and civil society. It isn't yet clear what will replace the disintegrating Age of Association institutions that once provided containers for community, trust-building relationships, and shared purpose. Social media has in many ways moved in to fill that vacuum, but it provides platforms for very different kinds of connections and discourse, with algorithms calibrated largely to inflame outrage and grievance, not belonging and togetherness.

Even more fundamentally, our previously shared stories no longer unite us. Long-held cultural narratives that once provided a unifying sense of identity and shared purpose have been called into question. Some of these narratives were questionable at best. For instance, the myth of perpetual progress and the perfectibility of humankind through education and technological development that brought such optimism in post-Enlightenment culture no longer seems plausible to many. Some of the people who were most committed to those foundational stories now exhibit deep pessimism about society's prospects. The myths of unfettered economic growth must contend with the downsides of environmental devastation and unsustainability.

The "great resignation" of workers across industries that emerged during the pandemic signifies that many people are reconsidering their sense of priorities. While it is a complex phenomenon with many causes, these employees are choosing to step away from positions, careers, and established systems, sometimes without a backup plan or safety net. They are reevaluating how they spend their time, how hard they want to work, what their work-life balance should be, and what it all means. For many, this is a sign of the spiritual estrangement they were experiencing, a sense of restlessness with the status quo, and a commitment to discover new and more life-giving patterns. It isn't clear what these trends will ultimately mean for society and where they will lead.

## Where People Are Looking

Following the apostles' stay with Lydia in Philippi in Acts 16, they kept traveling. Paul made it to Athens, where he went to the marketplace to talk with whoever was there, including the philosophers. Paul's proclamation led to him being taken into custody and brought before the local council on Mars Hill, where they asked to learn more about what he was saying. Paul responded with this thoughtful statement about religious plurality: "Athenians, I see how extremely spiritual you are in every way. For as I went through the city and looked carefully at the objects of your worship, I found among them an altar with the inscription, 'To an unknown god.' What therefore you worship as unknown, this I proclaim to you" (Acts 17:22–23).

If Paul were wandering around contemporary towns and cities, he could make the same comment. Even though institutional religious affiliation and participation are diminishing, religious impulses saturate contemporary culture. The quests for purity, righteousness, belonging, healing, and hope are as alive as ever, but these virtues are mostly expressed in secular forms. The religious drive to define who is elect/chosen and who is reprobate/condemned plays out in political and cultural tribalism. Politics is the new religion, functioning with key texts, prophets, insider language, practices of confession and forgiveness, assemblies, and rituals—especially on the extremes of right and left. For increasing numbers of Americans, these political/ideological identities are becoming their primary way of understanding themselves.[10]

Spiritual practices shorn of their religious roots, such as meditation and yoga, flourish in secularized form in popular culture. The Calm app, which provides guidance for meditation, has been downloaded by over one hundred million people. Fitness clubs such as SoulCycle offer a form of spiritualized community with regular practices and accountability. The impulse toward purity is channeled through food, diet, and consumer choices, where people seek cleanliness by eating vegan, buying organic, and so on. Concerts and nightclubs become rituals of communal bonding and euphoria. Rather than sit in church and listen to sermons, people turn to Ted Talks or podcasts for inspiration. These activities aren't inherently wrong in and of themselves, but for many people, they seem to be filling the place once held by God and religion.

Technology opens up further avenues. Smartphones make countless options accessible at everyone's fingertips that offer semblances of meaning, hope, inspiration, or the promise of connection. When anything from anywhere in the world that is available digitally is fair game, there is no reason to adhere to the congregation or denomination of one's family or local community. Some of these forms involve strong communal commitments and relationships, but many don't. Much of it is fundamentally transactional—companies sell the promise of spiritual meaning, purity, and so on through consumer purchases.

In the end, these options fail to deliver on their promises of providing human flourishing. With the countless choices available, there is no need to live within an intellectually or theologically coherent framework. Such coherence seems elusive—even in people's experiences of church. Anything that serves the individualized spiritual journey can be incorporated or discarded along the way. At the center of this quest is not the accumulated wisdom passed down through generations in a community but the individual self, which functions as the ultimate decider of truth and goodness. Yet from a Christian perspective, the human self is marred by brokenness. It is a shaky foundation upon which to build a civilization without the tempering influences of community, shared divine wisdom, habits, and norms that span generations and cultures.

## What Difference Does the Gospel Make?

The Lydias of today inhabit some version of this world. So what does the church have to offer her? How might Jesus matter to her search for wholeness and hope? The churches that are thriving have figured out how to connect the treasures of the gospel with what keeps Lydia up at night. They have made a turn toward prioritizing

everyday life, removing the divide between the sacred and the secular and seeing God's presence in all spaces. They are listening to
what their members and neighbors care about rather than focusing
on their own institutional problems.

> " The churches that are thriving have figured out how to connect the
> treasures of the gospel with what keeps Lydia up at night. "

To the extent to which churches' primary messages to members
and neighbors concentrate on institutional affiliation, participation, and support, they will continue to decline. To the extent to
which they learn how to join with Lydia, listen to her, and communicate the difference Jesus makes to her longings and losses, they will
discover new connections, energy, and hope. This isn't just a matter of concern for neighbors outside the church. This is essential for
those already within the pews as well.

Every Christian tradition will answer the question of what difference Jesus makes in today's culture in its own way. We invite you to
articulate how your tradition might speak into Lydia's longings and
losses, discovering the rich voices and practices within your community's heritage that can speak afresh today. We want to offer some
initial thoughts on how the gospel might address the contemporary
spiritual crisis. This is our brief version of answering the question,
*Why church?*

- *The world is both good and broken:* God created the world in
  all its beauty and complexity and set humanity within it to
  care for it. Having the freedom to choose, humans often
  choose wrongly, leading to a world marred by broken

relationships. The church is a community where followers of Jesus learn and rehearse the story of God's creation, remembering God's purposes for humankind and the world, and also wrestle honestly with the world's brokenness.

- *Life is communal:* In a time of acute loneliness, the God known in Jesus is a God of community. Christians talk about this as the Trinity—that God in Godself (ultimate reality) is a community of persons sharing a common life. Humans were created for community with God and one another. When we die, we're not alone: heaven is communal. The church is a community of people from every tribe and nation who discover a new unity in Christ.

- *It's not all up to you:* You have an identity as a child of God that you can neither earn nor lose. Your worth is dependent not on your actions and choices but upon God having chosen you. You don't need to write your own story; you can find yourself in a bigger story of God and of God's people through the ages. The church—the community of the followers of Jesus—can help you discover your place in that story.

- *You are not alone in your suffering:* Jesus entered into the worst places in human experience so we would know that God does not abandon us there. God raised Jesus from the dead as a tangible sign that injustice, torture, violence, and oppression are not ultimate. The church bears this promise of God's victory over the powers of evil and suffering.

- *Human flourishing is found in unconditional love and sacrificial service:* Jesus reached out to all manner of people, especially those excluded by society, with forgiveness and love. He did not hoard power but freely gave his very self to empower others. This love frees us to live sacrificially so that all may thrive. The church is the community in which we learn to practice this love in the here and now.

- *Your past doesn't define your future:* There is nothing that you have done that cannot be forgiven and released by God. In Christ, we become new creations. In God's Spirit, we are united across social and cultural differences into a new community of hope.

Why does the church matter? It bears in the gospel the most life-giving answer to the questions people are asking. In cities, towns, and neighborhoods across the world, there are people dying of isolation and despair. People are suffering profoundly without knowing God's love embodied in Jesus. They are living in narratives that divide, estrange, demean themselves or others, and lead to recurring cycles of enmity and retribution. They cannot identify a source of hope or a means of forgiving themselves or others. These are matters of life and death. The stakes are high for the church to communicate its unique story.

## Learning to Listen to God and Lydia

We now turn toward the steps of the faithful innovation journey. We will begin by exploring simple practices that can help the church listen more deeply to God and Lydia. We can discover a hopeful path forward by focusing not on the institutional church and its problems but rather on God's promises in Scripture, our own stories of God's presence in our lives, and God's movement among our neighbors. We invite you for the time being to set aside the institutional dilemmas your church may be facing, not because they aren't real and don't need to be addressed, but because the best way to address them is first to learn to be led by God into deeper connections with one another and our neighbors.

Each step in the faithful innovation journey is dependent upon prayer. God is at the center of this process, and we encourage a posture of continually seeking God's guidance at every stage. It is worth noting again that Lydia was found at "a place of prayer" (Acts 16:13). Prayer is the gateway to learning to love both God and our neighbors. The simple, concrete practices in the next three chapters will lay out a path by which you can draw closer to God and Lydia.

# Two

## Listen

Yvette was sitting on the morning train headed to work. Headphones in, phone in hand, and surrounded by people, she was listening to a podcast on how to start a small business. This was the part of the day she loved the most. This was her time—time when she could listen to whatever she wanted to during her thirty-minute commute. She always noticed that listening to something positive in the morning transformed her whole day. So she looked for encouraging and positive content, something to help her become the best version of herself. Yvette never really interacted with any of the people around her on the train. Most of them were also listening to something or engaged with their phones. But once in a while, Yvette would pause to wonder what the people around her were listening to and where they were going. She'd get curious about what might be happening in each of their lives.

---

Faithful innovation begins with listening. We need to listen to God, listen to one another, and listen to the people we encounter every day—our neighbors. By listening carefully to our everyday contexts and paying attention to the ways God may already be present in our own lives and the lives of the people around us, we discover how God is inviting us to be part of what God is already doing that we would have otherwise missed.

The steps in the faithful innovation process are simple: Listen, Act, and Share. We will unpack these three steps in each of the next three chapters so you can try them with the people in your own congregation. We'll include accessible practices and how-to guidance because the steps of the faithful innovation process are meant to be worked out in your ministry context.

> " The steps in the faithful innovation process are simple: Listen, Act, and Share. "

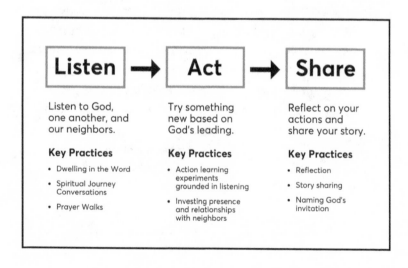

| Listen → | Act → | Share |
|---|---|---|
| Listen to God, one another, and our neighbors. | Try something new based on God's leading. | Reflect on your actions and share your story. |
| **Key Practices** | **Key Practices** | **Key Practices** |
| • Dwelling in the Word | • Action learning experiments grounded in listening | • Reflection |
| • Spiritual Journey Conversations | | • Story sharing |
| • Prayer Walks | • Investing presence and relationships with neighbors | • Naming God's invitation |

Despite their simplicity, though, these steps are not easy. We have collaborated with hundreds of churches in multiple denominations to design a simple yet meaningful way for congregations to learn how to follow God's leading together.[1] The journey of Listen-Act-Share addresses a question that congregations everywhere are asking: *We know our church needs to change, but we're not sure what to do.* Maybe your church is wondering this too. Many people in communities of faith would like to see their church thrive, but they aren't sure what they can do beyond the ways they are already serving. As we walked beside leaders and their congregations, a fundamental question kept emerging: *How do we find a new way to be the church in the twenty-first century?*

## Starting with Listening

Listening is a very practical first step in this journey. It is not passive; it is active. It involves exploring your environment both inside and outside of the church. Listening involves learning to walk (or bike or drive) around your neighborhood while asking God to help you see what God sees in that place. It includes inviting people in your congregation to share stories about when they have felt most spiritually alive and connected to God. Listening involves building relationships with the people around you every day and asking them to share, if they are comfortable, what their own spiritual journeys have been like in their lives. Maybe most importantly, listening involves reading Scripture together with others and wondering about what God might be saying to you collectively. These simple-to-understand but sometimes hard-to-do practices change the conversation from *How do we fix our church?* to *Where do we notice God in our everyday lives?* This signals a movement from "church questions" to "God questions." With listening, the conversation shifts from talking about institutional survival to learning how to join in the work God is doing in the world.

> " *With listening, the conversation shifts from talking about institutional survival to learning how to join in the work God is doing in the world.* "

When you begin to listen, you start to notice things that never caught your attention before. You might see God doing something unexpected, in an unusual place or through an unusual person. You might be surprised by the ways God is working, especially if they don't fit how you understand God. Sometimes, the things God shows you are an invitation for you—and for the members of your congregation—to personally or collectively join God in that work. What you hear and observe might press you to consider whether you and the people in your community are ready to trust God by stepping out in faith and trying something new.

## Listening for Lydia

Listening to God isn't always easy or clear. In the Acts 16 story, Paul and his companions were searching for people who were open to hearing the good news they felt God had directed them to share. They were listening for God's leading as they traveled from town to town. The group went to several places where they thought God was leading them to share the good news about Jesus, only to find out that once they arrived, they weren't able to connect with the people there. Their path wasn't straight, and they had to wonder at times if they were completely wrong about what God was asking them to do. Acts 16:7 even says that when they tried to enter Bithynia, "the Spirit of Jesus did not allow them." While Paul and his team thought they were in the right place doing what God wanted them to do, God's Spirit led them in a totally different direction.

Once they came to Samothrace, Paul had a dream of a man from Macedonia. The man in the dream begged Paul to come there and help him. The next morning, Paul and his companions concluded that this dream was God speaking to them, inviting them to go locate the Macedonian man. They responded by packing their things and setting out. But when they arrived in Macedonia, they couldn't find the man from the dream. They had to wonder whether they'd misheard what God was trying to tell them. Was the dream really from God? Did Paul eat some bad food the night before that caused the dream? Were they really in the right place?

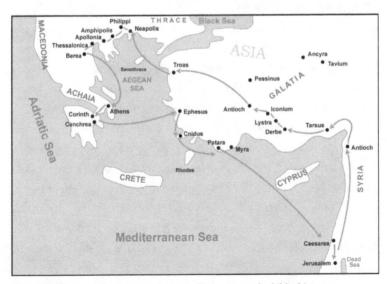

Map of Paul's second missionary journey. From geography.bible-history.com.

Paul and his companions decided to go outside the city to a place of prayer and see what might happen there. Near the river, they met a group of women who were seeking a connection with God but who had never heard about Jesus. This is where they first encountered Lydia. She was a leader among the assembled women, and she engaged with Paul as he shared the good news about Jesus with her. But here's the curious thing: Lydia was not a *man* from Macedonia. She was a businesswoman from Thyatira. As we look closely at the Acts 16 story, it becomes clear that *Lydia* is who God intended for Paul and his companions to meet. Their path to her was neither obvious nor straightforward. They had to zigzag their way through several other cities to eventually come across the person God intended them to find.

This kind of careful, prayerful, and attentive listening to God requires patience and the understanding that we might have to try a few things before we discover what God is calling us to do. We've seen what can happen in congregations when they remain open and curious about wherever God might be leading them. One congregational team member had been practicing Dwelling in the Word (a simple practice of listening to God through Scripture, which we will describe below) using Acts 16 with his congregational guiding team. One Saturday, as he was driving to pick up his dry cleaning, he went past a low-income apartment building and saw people gathering outside with tables and chairs. Normally, he would have driven right past. But because he had been engaged in the story of the disciples looking for God's leading in Acts 16, he turned around, parked his car, and walked up. He asked what was going on. Everyone said, "You have to talk to Rita." Eventually, he found Rita, a resident there who hosted a monthly meal for the neighborhood. She invited him to join them, which he did, allowing him to hear these neighbors' stories. He realized that Rita was like Lydia in Acts 16—a person of peace in the neighborhood through whom he could make deeper connections. What started as an errand ended up becoming an opportunity to draw close to neighbors because his imagination was shaped by the practice of listening to God through Scripture.

## Listening to God and Others

The act of listening happens in the context of community. Whether we are listening to God, listening to the people in our care, or listening to our neighbors in the world around us, we need the presence of others to make this activity possible. Even when we are listening to our own selves—paying attention to our own thoughts and needs—we are never truly alone. God is present with us, serving as our listening partner regardless of whether we are able to discern God's presence. As our friend and colleague Scott Cormode reminds us, "Leadership begins with listening."[2] We as leaders begin our listening by surrounding ourselves with people to whom, and with whom, we can listen.

Paul is the type of leader who exemplifies the ability to listen to God and to others. When he embarked on his second missionary journey, he was not traveling by himself. Paul did decide to part ways with Barnabas over the disagreement about Mark, whose previous desertion made Paul unwilling to bring him along (Acts 15:36–39). But instead of going forth alone after the split, he chose Silas to accompany him as he set out for Syria and Cilicia (Acts 15:40–41). Timothy joined them soon afterward (Acts 16:1–4), and the trio continued on to Phrygia, Galatia, and Troas (Acts 16:6–8).

The apostle beautifully models listening to God through the dream of the man in Macedonia. It's clear that Paul wasn't the only one who was carefully and thoughtfully listening to God as he received the dream. Paul listened to God's instructions to take the next faithful step on the journey, but he tested that new direction with his companions, who listened and agreed to take this next step together. Although Paul was the direct recipient of God's message through a dream, his friends became recipients, too, when they decided to interrupt their plans and move in the direction God wanted them to take. Paul experienced the Spirit's intervention. He and his companions responded willingly, and they became participants in God's mission as they listened to God and sought to honor God by taking the dream seriously. There is a perceptible sense of energy and dynamism in how quickly they set out.

## The Role of the Holy Spirit in Listening

For ministry leaders, a central aspect of listening is helping a community learn to hear what the Spirit of God is doing in its midst. The Holy Spirit may speak to any member of the community, in any role or position. Receiving and interpreting these messages leads to response, allowing God to shape our ministry plans and activities. Doing the complicated work of ministry without the leading of the Spirit is a sure recipe for burnout. We were never intended to lead God's church on our own without the sustaining power of God.

If we have just our own energy to guide us, we'll quickly get bogged down in the mundane tasks of running and sustaining a church structure. These never-ending responsibilities might range from making decisions about church programs and balancing the budget to resolving conflicts, maintaining the building, and more. These activities helpfully support the work of ministry. But when they eclipse the core spiritual work of the church, they can become soul-draining distractions. On their own, these things don't address the actual mission of the church as God designed it—to make Christian disciples and to reach the world with the gospel message of Jesus Christ. Yet the church landscape is littered with congregations that have lost clarity on their spiritual purpose—their call to participate in God's creative, healing, restoring work in their context—and instead are consumed with managing and sustaining a religious institution. No wonder leaders feel ground down. The necessary managerial work becomes far more life-giving when grounded in spiritual clarity, focus, and presence.

When God's Spirit is welcomed into our midst, the real work of discipleship moves within reach. What may have seemed humanly impossible before becomes divinely possible as God opens the doors. God travels the road beside us too. Paul's team of missionaries had another unseen member. The Spirit of God that announced their journey accompanied them on the trip, going ahead of them and preparing Lydia for their arrival (Acts 16:14). God was not just giving them directions; God was actively participating in the process.

## Simple Listening Practices

At the heart of the faithful innovation journey are simple, ancient spiritual practices that help us focus on God's presence and activity in our lives. We develop affection for whatever captures our attention—whatever we allow to fill our time. Spiritual practices shift our attention to God. They are tools that place us in God's presence so God can do transforming work within us. When we focus on God by carefully listening not only to God but also to one another and our neighbors, this is one way that we can concretely express our love for God.

> " At the heart of the faithful innovation journey are simple, ancient spiritual practices that help us focus on God's presence and activity in our lives. "

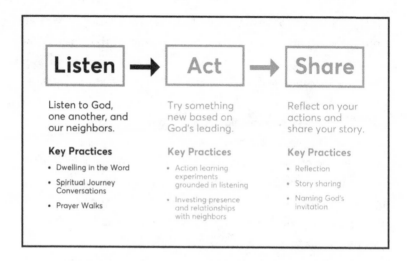

Here are three listening practices you can try with your congregation as the first step in your faithful innovation journey: Dwelling in the Word, Spiritual Journey Conversations, and Prayer Walks.

Dwelling in the Word[3] is an ancient practice of listening to a passage from the Bible with a group of people. It creates space to allow the biblical text to speak to us and help us interpret what is happening in our lives and in the world. You choose a passage of Scripture that might help you process something happening in the life of your congregation. An example is Acts 16:6–15 for learning how God leads us to new places and people. After you pray for God to speak, have two different people read the passage aloud twice, pausing for silent reflection after each reading. Consider what catches your imagination in the passage, what questions the passage raises for you, and what God *might* be saying to you as a group through the passage. Notice that the language around this question leaves room for ambiguity as to the nature of God's message. Invite everyone to pair up with a "reasonably friendly looking stranger" and spend three to four minutes each sharing what caught your imagination or what you wondered about. Then reassemble everyone as a large group (or in smaller groups of six to eight) and ask people to share one thing they heard their partner say about the text. This becomes an exercise in careful listening to the other person as well as listening to God through the text. As you discuss your responses together, first in pairs and then as a large group, themes or insights may emerge that are relevant to whatever your community is going through.

> Dwelling in the Word invites you to consider three key questions as you listen to a passage of Scripture together: *What catches your imagination in this passage? What questions does this passage raise for you? What might God be saying to you as a group through this passage?*

The practice of Dwelling in the Word can be used repeatedly, returning to a single passage or multiple passages over time. The repetition helps the group become more attentive to how God speaks to us collectively through the Bible. Congregations that do this become more comfortable at naming ways they sense God leading them through the text. This practice directs us toward what we think God might be encouraging us to do in our church rather than just our own ideas about best practices and next steps. Sometimes our thoughts and God's leading are the same things, but often, they are not. We need practices that prioritize God's direction over our own impulses.

Spiritual Journey Conversations give people a chance to share stories about times in their lives when they have felt most spiritually alive. These conversations are both simple and intentional, and they open space for people to talk about aspects of their spiritual journey that they might not normally have the opportunity to share. The practice works best when you give people a few questions to ask one another, either while they are gathered together or when they are on their own. People tell their stories in pairs, and then they are invited to consider and identify how God may have been present in these important moments. We give them "God questions" to ask of their own stories, such as the following:

- What do you think God might have been doing at this time in your life?
- Was God teaching you something? Was God reassuring or encouraging you?
- Was God challenging you? Was God inviting you into something?

This practice accomplishes two things simultaneously: it builds community as people learn about one another's stories, and it builds our ability to see where God has been active in all of our lives.

> Spiritual Journey Conversations invite people to share stories by asking, *What was happening in your life during a time you felt most spiritually alive? What energized you most during this time? Did the church play a role in this experience, and if so, how?*

At one of our congregational trainings, a group of longtime friends from the church was invited to share some Spiritual Journey Conversations with one another. These members had raised their families together in the church over the past thirty years. After they had participated in the exercise, the group of four women came up to us to share what a powerful experience that was for them. They commented that despite having known one another for so many years and participating in church together, they had never heard the stories their friends had each shared that day. They discovered how taking the time to really listen can profoundly deepen and enrich our relationships.

Prayer Walks are another ancient practice of simply paying attention to particular places. We ask God to help us see what God sees and to hear what God hears. Prayer Walks are far less intimidating than they sound. This isn't proselytizing your neighborhood. Instead, this is the spiritual act of paying attention to your surroundings—this could be where you work, where you live, where you worship, or even where you shop. You could even do this practice in the places where you spend time online. Wherever you find yourself each week is the right place for a Prayer Walk.

Here are a few steps to help you try this spiritual practice. First, determine a time and place to walk, and invite people to walk with you. Consider printing a map of the area or having one ready on your phone. Make a plan for how far you will walk and in which direction you will go. Begin with a reminder of the goals of the Prayer Walk—paying attention to your surroundings and asking God to help you see what God sees. Be ready to pray for things as you encounter them. God might prompt you to pray for peace and justice in the neighborhood, provision for neighbors' needs, or other themes like forgiveness, healing, protection, and opportunity. You can stop and pray aloud together, pray silently as you continue to walk, and pray for people you come across. You needn't fear offering to pray for someone you meet on your walk. If you ask respectfully, the person can always say no. People often say yes; you might be surprised by how open people are to having others pray for them.

When you are done with your walk, stop and pray a closing prayer with your group. Ask those with you if anything from your walk seems particularly important. Consider together if there is anything you noticed that God might be inviting you to spend more time learning about in the future. Thank God for being with you on your walk.

> Prayer Walks help us pay attention to our physical environment by asking these questions: *Who is around you and what are they doing? What catches your attention and makes you want to learn more? What do you think God might be doing in this place?*

## God Is Already in the Neighborhood

Incredible things happen when congregations commit to being present in and praying for the spaces around them. A group of people from an urban church went on a Prayer Walk in a neighborhood near where the church worshipped. Many of them had never been on a Prayer Walk before. They were probably wondering things like, *What do you even do on a Prayer Walk? Do you pray out loud the whole time you are walking? Do you pray for people on the street? Do you just pray silently as you walk?* These are understandable questions, and as the church group created a plan for where they were going to walk, they decided their goal would be to pay careful attention to what was around them as they traveled together. They remained open to letting God reveal important observations about the neighborhood.

The church team encountered different parts of the landscape now that they were walking instead of driving, including a couple of large apartment buildings. One of the buildings had a reception desk near the entrance, so they went in to inquire about how the building was used. The staff member told them the building was part of a local organization focused on providing affordable housing for people who were experiencing HIV/AIDS. It was a low-profile, private residence where people sharing similar experiences could live together in community with the goal of promoting health and safety. The people from the church who first learned about the building returned to the congregation and shared their discoveries. As more groups conducted Prayer Walks, all of the teams shared what they were noticing so everyone could benefit from their listening work in the neighborhood.

A few months later, the church got a call from the affordable housing organization asking if people from the congregation could provide Christmas gift bags for their residents with gloves, hats, other basic essentials, and cookies. While the organization made it clear the church couldn't include Bibles or any material advertising the church, the congregation saw this as an opportunity to love their neighbors. They agreed to provide the bags.

As time passed, the people from the church began to feel as though God was leading them to explore the possibility of building relationships with the residents. They asked for permission to offer a monthly meal. The building had a community room that was designed for communal meals, so the church asked if they could host it there to make it easier for people to come. The building director said yes. Soon, a group of faithful church members regularly hosted the meal. Over many months, the turnout varied. Sometimes many residents came, and sometimes just a few turned up. The church group wondered if the monthly meal program was effective. But they kept doing it because they believed God wanted them to continue building relationships.

Months later, the local neighborhood association called the church to ask for help. They were trying to survey all of the people who lived in the area to determine how excess funding from a budget surplus should be spent. The neighborhood association had heard that the church had relationships with the residents in this building. They had been unable to get them to respond, and they wanted to make sure their voices were included.

The congregation was ready to act. When the neighborhood association offered several thousand dollars, the church used the money to host an outdoor party in the building's courtyard. It was open to everyone, with food, games, and even a puppet show. Many residents came and many filled out the survey. The church members were amazed at the opportunity they felt like God gave them through this moment. The neighborhood they prayed for and walked through had reached out to them, offering them funding to ensure that often-overlooked voices were heard. What started with a Prayer Walk had culminated into life-giving relationships. All this transpired because a few people noticed the building and took steps to explore what was happening there.

The story didn't end there. Relationships continued to grow between the residents and people from the church. Some residents came to worship at the church. When one of the residents passed away, one of the pastors was invited to provide a memorial service for him at the building. Many people from the building attended and heard about his Christian faith.

It was a tremendous honor for the church to help create a space where this person's life could be celebrated by those who cared about him. The congregation saw how God had clearly invited them into this community to learn from the residents and also demonstrate God's love for them. It can sometimes be hard to discern whether to keep doing something, and the early volunteers persevered because they perceived God's call. We never know how God might use a practice like a Prayer Walk to open up opportunities for relationship and ministry. Listening for God's leading often does not follow a straight line. Instead, God calls our attention to people and places that we may never have noticed. This is an important part of the faithful innovation journey.

## Cultivating Space for God's Story

Ministry leaders help their people learn how to listen carefully for what God might want to do among them. This means cultivating practices by which the people can grow in their ability to listen to and be led by God. Like Paul, it may begin with identifying an inner circle of people. These key leaders, like Paul's missionary companions, can join you in guiding your congregants toward understanding and practicing the art of listening. You want your people to grasp the importance of listening for the movement of the Holy Spirit as part of the ongoing and regular life of the church.

The practice of listening goes in both directions. While leaders must pay attention to how God is guiding them on behalf of the community, they must also listen to God through the voices of those they serve. Central to this work is the *interpretive* dimension of leadership, in which leaders gather the voices and threads of the community's discernment into a shared story.[4] In practice, this means cultivating practices of prayer, storytelling, and listening within the congregation and, as people share publicly what they're hearing, naming the key themes that emerge. Leaders can reflect these themes back to the community in order to test them, asking, *Is this what we're hearing?* As the community affirms and refines these interpretations, greater clarity emerges around God's call. This is an iterative and ongoing process.

## Challenges of Listening to God and Others

The Christian practices we use to help us listen might appear simple. Yet we need to acknowledge how hard the act of listening can be. It seems like listening should be fairly straightforward, but there are layers of possible challenges that arise. For instance, the very language of saying that we're "listening to God" makes some people uncomfortable. They might protest that it seems kind of arrogant to think we can actually hear what God might be saying. Even if we *could* hear from God, they'd argue, how would we be sure we understand the message?

Church traditions play a role in how comfortable people are with the idea of God speaking to us. For some denominations, this kind of talk is quite foreign to their understanding of God. Yet for others, their traditions are steeped in experiences of hearing directly from God on a regular basis. No matter where you find yourself on the Christian spectrum, the truth is that our finite humanity limits our perception of God. We can't ever be 100 percent sure we're hearing—or understanding—what God might be trying to tell us.

For this reason, we need to use lots of qualifiers when we talk about hearing from God. Our language matters. It's better to say "God *might* be saying this" or "It's *possible* God wants us to pay closer attention to this issue" than to frame our statements with "God said" or "God told me." This models vulnerability and a humility that we are open to differing interpretations of what we heard. The key here is that we don't need to have absolute certainty about God's message before we move in the direction God appears to be leading us. When we use words like "might," "maybe," and "possibly," we open up dialogue with one another. This practice allows the community to work together to determine what God might be saying to us.

We also weigh what we might be hearing from God against what we know is true about God from Scripture. If what we think God is saying to us aligns with the biblical narrative, and if it encourages us to love God and love our neighbors, then we can proceed with greater confidence.

Another challenge to listening is the noise in our everyday lives. This isn't just the physical sounds of our environments either. We are bombarded with information and media in ways that would have been inconceivable for previous generations. Our most precious resource in the twenty-first century is arguably our attention, largely because so many entities are fighting to capture it. From the moment we wake up, already reaching for our phones, to the moment we go to bed, something or someone is trying to occupy our focus. We have an important choice to make. What we pay attention to, and what we decide to ignore, influences who we are becoming as human beings. Who or what are we allowing to shape us?

Finally, our overscheduled and harried lives don't leave much room for the practice of listening. Most of us simply don't have space in our days that we can dedicate to listening to others. Think about your own average day or week. As a regular practice, do you have time set aside for just listening to your friends, your coworkers, your partner, or your kids? If, for example, your neighbor wants to tell you a twenty-minute story about something that happened to her, will you be able to listen? We know a pastor who tries to always leave her house at least ten to fifteen minutes early so she has room for random conversations with neighbors. This is a variation of the spiritual practice of simplicity. This pastor is making space in her day that God can fill. Imagine what God might be able to accomplish with that time!

> Simplicity is about being wise stewards of our time so God can better utilize us for God's mission in the world. We say no to good things so we can say yes to even better things. We let God's priorities determine how we spend our days.

Certain cultural contexts are much better at creating this kind of space for listening and relationships than others. Regrettably, the busy schedules that are prevalent in many Western cultures prevent us from taking the time to listen deeply to one another. In much of the United States, listening is a rare art. Many people do not regularly experience the profound connection of someone else sitting down with them, looking them in the eyes, and giving them their full attention. This life-changing practice can have an impact in as little as five minutes.

It would seem like the church is a good venue for listening, but the problem prevails even there. The common rhythms of congregational life, which emphasize scheduled programming, prevent this kind of listening from happening. The practice of listening is only possible when the church is intentional about making space for it. While this takes planning and effort, the outcomes are worth it. When we've given people opportunities to have Spiritual Journey Conversations with one another in the churches we've worked with, many of them have told us afterward that it was the first time they'd been given the chance to share their stories in church. What would happen in our churches if we created space in the worship services and small group gatherings for people to simply share their life stories together?

We invite you to consider this outside the church too. There is often no natural, regular, ongoing way for people in congregations to listen to the people who are outside the church. There's no easy way to engage them in the kinds of core questions we've been talking about. Do we have space in our everyday lives where we can invite our neighbors—people who aren't part of a congregation—to tell their stories about their spiritual backgrounds and journeys, to share their questions about how to make meaning out of life, and to explore their worries, doubts, and fears that sometimes keep them up at night? If we don't have that kind of opportunity regularly, how will we ever know how God might already be present in the lives of these neighbors? We can't just wait until they show up for worship. Unless we go where they are, our paths might not ever cross.

## Waiting for God

One of the most challenging parts of this first step in the faithful innovation process is the amount of patience it requires. When you begin intentionally listening, you don't know *when* you might notice or hear something that God intends to use to direct your path. This rarely happens immediately. So you have to keep listening patiently, trusting that God will eventually show you which way to go.

There have been many times in our own leadership journeys when we wondered how long we should wait in a particular place or with a particular group of people. We didn't always know whether to keep doing a particular activity or program or if we should continue waiting for God to reveal something. You have to learn to trust your collective ability—the discernment of your leadership team—to know when God might be telling you to move on to the next thing. It's normal for listening to feel ambiguous. It was ambiguous for Paul and his companions in Acts 16. But they kept listening and taking the next step, and they did it together.

> " It's normal for listening to feel ambiguous. "

Michael was part of planting a church that worshipped at a public school on Sunday mornings. He volunteered to serve on a local board called a "site council" at school, where he went to monthly meetings to learn about what was happening at the school—budgets, events, parent involvement, and more. He was there to contribute wherever he could and also listen on behalf of the congregation. The church had wondered how and if God wanted them to be part of what God was already doing at the school.

After one of the meetings, the principal asked to speak to Michael. She told him that the administration was trying to address a problem. Students were stealing food from the cafeteria on Fridays. She said the theft was happening because the kids were experiencing food insecurity. They weren't sure whether they would have enough food to get through the weekends. Then the principal asked Michael the pivotal question: *Is there anything the church can do to help us address this problem?*

The church community had been praying about serving the school in a way that really mattered *to them*. The church didn't want to take on a project that simply made the congregation feel useful. They wanted their efforts to be valuable to everyone at the school—the teachers, administration, staff, and students. When Michael heard this question from the principal, he knew this was God's invitation. The church had listened for months for God's leading. When it finally came, they were ready. Michael shared the question with others in the congregation, and everyone agreed this was something God was inviting them into. They began experimenting with ways to address the kids' needs by putting food in their back-packs on Fridays before the weekend. This experiment became a programmatic effort to offer food to any student in the school who needed it. After developing the program for over a year, a few people in the congregation discerned that God was inviting them to try it in other schools. Eventually, the church launched its own nonprofit, which currently serves hundreds of schools in its local community. All of this began with intentional listening for God's invitation and a willingness to experiment with a new way of joining God's work.

## Discovering the Path

One of the best ways to practice listening is to find companions for the journey. Paul didn't do this work alone and neither should we. Start by forming a small team of trusted people who want to enter the faithful innovation process with you. This could be a group of three or four people who are willing to try out some of the practices from this chapter in their own lives. This team could also volunteer to inter-view people inside and outside of the church to find out what matters to them. Listening works best when we hear from a wide range of people. Use your team to encourage others in the congregation to try some of these practices and also to begin listening to one another and to their neighbors. While it can be challenging to listen to people who are different from us, that kind of listening can be transforma-tive, as we learn to see how God is at work in unexpected people and places. The more people who are doing the listening, and the more people who are being heard, the more the congregation can be part of what God is doing.

Listening together alongside others in our community helps us start to follow our spiritual instincts about where God may want us to go next. You might be wondering, *What does God's leading sound like to other people who have done this before?* Some of God's promptings are small things, like listening to a neighbor. Others are much bigger challenges, like starting a new ministry or engaging with people who are different from you. God knows where we need to start and invites us to take our next step. Here are examples of these kinds of spiritual hunches others have developed through careful listening:

- Maybe God is inviting us to create more time in our lives to get to know our neighbors.
- Maybe God is calling us to build relationships with people who live near our church building.
- Maybe God is calling us to ask people for their prayer requests.
- Maybe God is calling us to address the injustices people are experiencing in our neighborhood.
- Maybe God is inviting us to get invited over to our neighbor's house.
- Maybe God is inviting us to learn how to talk about why our faith matters to us in ways other people can easily understand.
- Maybe God is calling us to help feed people in our area who are experiencing food insecurity.
- Maybe God is calling us to start a new expression of church.
- Maybe God is calling us to build relationships with people who are different from us.
- Maybe God is calling us to listen to people with other religious backgrounds.
- Maybe God is inviting us to help create more housing for people experiencing homelessness.
- Maybe God is inviting us to . . .

Listening is the first step in the faithful innovation process. But there is more. If you only engage in listening practices, you will miss out on actually meeting the Lydias in your life. We need to find ways to *try* new things based on what we learn from our listening. The next step in our journey teaches us to act on what we've learned from our listening. Trying something new changes our mindset; it helps us "behave our way into new thinking."[5] In the next chapter, we will walk through the creation of action learning experiments with your congregation.

# Three

## Act

Marco lived down the street from Main Street Church. He had never attended any sort of religious services growing up, and now faith just seemed too odd to him. He worked as a rideshare driver, ferrying passengers to and from the airport, and picked up seasonal construction jobs whenever he could. Marco didn't feel like any part of his life was particularly worthy of attention. He was pretty certain that the church would have no use for someone like him. Then one afternoon, he noticed someone sitting in a lawn chair outside by the entrance to the church building. It kept happening every few days—different people were there for hours at a time, basking in the afternoon sun and talking to whoever walked by. Marco was suddenly intrigued. Before he knew it, he was heading down the sidewalk toward the person in the chair to find out what was happening.

---

At the start of this book, we asserted that congregations are facing challenges with no easy answers. It takes more than a redesigned website, a new worship style, or a building remodel to address what's happening. Even hiring new leaders isn't enough. Fundamental changes are needed at the heart of the church. In other words, congregations must discover new ways to be the church in the twenty-first century. This kind of learning requires broad participation—it has to involve more than just the church leaders. The church as an institution needs to undergo a transformation so it can learn to forge fresh connections with people inside its walls and outside in the community. For many congregations, this is the core work. Change becomes possible as people engage in personal spiritual transformation that expands their imagination of what it means to be the church. This is why spiritual practices are so central to the faithful innovation process. The best way to learn about the practices is to do them. We invite you to do more than just think, talk, or even read about them. You have to experience them for yourself to discover how God desires to work through them and how they might

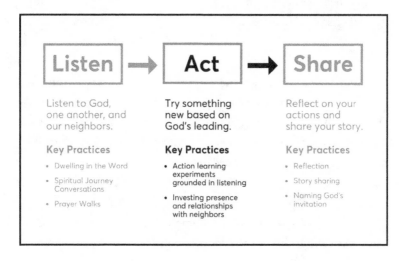

impact you. That's why the second step in the faithful innovation process invites us to Act.

This chapter focuses on what we call action learning experiments. This might sound complicated, but it simply means we are going to try some new things that we hope will help us learn how to follow God's leading and be the church. This approach has a bias toward action—rather than talking about the changes we need to make, we take steps to try something new. We define an experiment as a planned set of actions that help us behave our way into new thinking so we can learn how to address the challenges we are facing. Experiments are the best way forward when the problem we've encountered can't be solved by existing expertise or knowledge. This kind of challenge requires us to adapt and do something different from what we're used to doing.[1]

> " We define an experiment as a planned set of actions that help us behave our way into new thinking so we can learn how to address the challenges we are facing. "

Action learning experiments help us discover new ways to be the church in our context. An experiment's success is determined by how much we learn and are transformed rather than by how much impact our actions have on others. Experiments must be simple, repeatable, and affordable.

Think of action learning experiments as a spiritual practice. As the next step in the faithful innovation process, they are intended to help us go deeper and explore something God brought to our attention from our listening work. The process itself is cyclical and ongoing; for example, we continue to listen even as we begin to engage in experiments. Acting flows from listening, as what we hear influences and informs what we decide to try out in our contexts.

When we undertake new actions, this produces new learning that helps churches get a clearer picture of how God might be leading them. Wide participation is paramount: the more people who join the experiments, the more energy, enthusiasm, and buy-in there will be for the learning that comes out of them. Learning by doing is an essential way to discover how God is inviting the congregation to engage with the Lydias in their community.

## The Search for Lydia

Paul and his companions had to go to several different places before they found Lydia outside the city in Macedonia. Acts 16:6–8 describes how they went to Phrygia and Galatia, Bithynia, and Troas before they finally arrived in Macedonia. Even when they got to Macedonia, they had to go outside the city to find the person God had planned for them to meet. Paul's dream suggested they would look for a "man of Macedonia" (Acts 16:9), but God's Spirit led them to a woman. How did this group of Christ followers know that they should keep going? What kept them faithfully traveling to all of these places? Why didn't they just give up and go home when things got confusing?

Some members of this band of disciples had been trained by Jesus himself through experiences like we see recorded in Luke 10:1–12. Jesus sent out seventy-two disciples to visit towns "where he himself intended to go" (Luke 10:1). He gave them clear instructions about how to enter a town—they were to offer peace to people

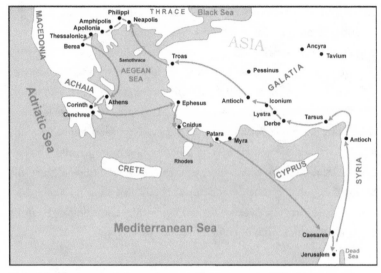

Map of Paul's second missionary journey. From geography.bible-history.com.

they met, receive hospitality from those who welcomed them, join in the life of the village, and proclaim the kingdom of God while offering healing. Anytime they were not welcomed or offered hospitality, Jesus told them to move on to the next place. This is exactly what Paul and his companions are doing in Acts 16. They are moving about from town to town, offering peace and looking for hospitality. They continued on to the next place when they didn't find any welcome from the people they met because they believed God intended for them to go somewhere else and share the gospel that Jesus entrusted to them.

This pattern of setting out, offering peace, searching for and receiving hospitality, and proclaiming the gospel is a very counter-cultural way of doing ministry for most Western congregations in the twenty-first century. Many congregations are used to doing the hosting, to extending hospitality to others rather than being the recipient. They often invest large amounts of time and resources to determine how they can become more hospitable to those who are new to their community. Yet few churches wonder how they might *receive* hospitality from their neighbors. This is far more uncomfortable and vulnerable. When people enter our church buildings, we control the activities, the food, and the overall feel of the space. Being hosted by someone else means relinquishing our comforts, preferences, and even expectations of the outcome. We have little idea of what will happen.

This is exactly what Paul and his companions did as they trusted God. They knew they were called by God to look for places where people might welcome them and receive the good news they had been commissioned by Jesus to share. They were equipped to share the gospel in both word and action, offering tangible healing to people who were suffering (Acts 16:16–18) and also sharing the truth about Jesus and his sacrifice for the sins of the world. They moved from place to place at the Spirit's prompting, never sure exactly what was about to happen but confident that God was preparing the way forward for them.

Churches often focus their energy on planning events or developing programs that they hope people will attend. We want to suggest a different way of being the church. What if God is calling us to leave the confines of our buildings—to go out and receive hospitality from our neighbors rather than offering it to them? What if we prioritized getting an invitation to our neighbor's home for dinner rather than only considering how we might invite people into our spaces, with our food and customary ways of being together? Jesus had a knack for inviting himself over to other people's houses; we believe this could be a profoundly transformative practice for congregations today. If we all committed to doing this, it would be a radical departure from the way churches have operated in the last century.

Paul and his companions in Acts 16 were clear on *what* they felt called to do. They believed God was sending them to share the good news of Jesus Christ in word and action with people outside the Jewish community. They were clear on *why* they were doing this too. They believed that the life, death, and resurrection of Jesus were life changing and world changing. They affirmed that the gift of Jesus was for everyone. They were driven by a desire to demonstrate the difference Jesus makes in the lives of people, and they had a sense of urgency to tell people who had not yet heard or responded to the gospel.

So they were clear on their *why* as well as their *what*. They were not clear on *how* they were going to do this. They didn't know exactly where they were going. They assumed that they would have to move about from place to place in order to discover where God wanted them to go. It wasn't possible for them to have committee meeting after committee meeting in hopes that their destination would suddenly become clear to them. They had to make a move and try something.

Following God's leading, this team of apostles first tried to preach the good news in the province of Asia. Acts 16:6–7 tells us that they attempted to enter several places, but the Spirit of God would not allow them. What in the world does that mean? We aren't given many details about how they figured out that God didn't want them to go to some of these locations, but they clearly understood that they needed to move on to another place.

This would be very difficult for many congregations today to accept. Imagine you spent a long time planning a new effort to reach your community or neighborhood. Maybe you identified a place in your city to host an event like an Easter egg hunt or a job fair or to offer an outdoor worship service. People from your congregation volunteered their time to bring this opportunity to life. Now imagine that the event is over, and it was not a "success." Not only did no one show up, but it was clear that the community didn't want you there. *How would your congregation respond?*

Many churches would interpret this kind of experience as a "failure." They might even assume they did something wrong. While that is a possibility, we want to suggest an alternative interpretation. What if this was the Spirit of God redirecting your congregation's energy? If you were able to recast the event in this light, would your congregation eagerly approach the next opportunity and say, *Where else might God be inviting us to try to engage in similar ways?* If not, would your congregation assume they shouldn't try again? Would the perception of failure keep them from acting?

Interpretation matters. The companions in Acts 16 saw their experiences as God's direction to search for hospitality somewhere else. They continued to look for places where the peace they offered would be received and welcomed. *They did not give up and go home.* They persevered. They didn't question their *what* or their *why*. They just kept innovating on the *how* by moving to the next place and trying again. They learned from their experiences and discerned together where they thought God might be leading them next. The Acts 16 narrative teaches us important lessons about how we follow God's leading into an unknown future.

## Faithfully Innovative Actions

So what are we supposed to *do*? This is a very common question that many congregations ask as they learn to faithfully innovate. We have already explored how to listen to God, one another, and our neighbors. Building upon that work, the next step is to design some simple action learning experiments that people in your congregation can try. The main purpose of action learning experiments is the learning and transformation of the people who participate in them. Experiments are not intended to immediately increase the number of people who are attending worship or considering membership. They are designed to help the congregation learn how to join God's work in the world. Experiments often involve investing our personal presence in some new places and investing in new relationships with the people around us. This includes sharing the gospel and helping our neighbors notice the difference Jesus makes in their lives. By learning through actions, congregations discover new ways to be the church and connect with people inside and outside of their walls. Experiments are the embodiment of innovation; they are about doing things we have never done before. Action learning experiments in particular are the primary spiritual practices for this part of the faithful innovation journey.

> " The main purpose of action learning experiments is the learning and transformation of the people who participate in them. "

An action learning experiment consists of three simple parts. First, we define what a group of people is trying to learn. This often arises out of our listening work in the first step. Maybe your congregation learned there is limited access to fresh produce in your community, so you want to know how to address food insecurity among your neighbors. Or maybe the people in your church noticed an influx of new residents nearby, so they are interested in learning about the newcomers' spiritual backgrounds and the questions they have about faith and spirituality. Perhaps you are curious about how God is already present in the lives of young people who aren't currently participating in your church. It is crucial to be clear about what you want to learn when you design an action learning experiment. If your work in this stage lacks clarity, you might end up trying something and being confused later about why you did it. Moreover, you won't be able to meet your desired objective if you don't know what it is. Having a carefully crafted goal will ensure that the design of your experiment will lead you in the direction you want to go.

Second, once you have defined what you want to learn, you can start to name the steps you will take in order to behave your way into new thinking. You are inviting people to try something with an ambiguous outcome. This will naturally generate some anxiety. It can be helpful at this stage to remind people that God takes care of the outcome. Your steps must also be extra clear to help manage the uncertainty that comes with experimentation. Jesus modeled this for us with his instructions to the disciples in Luke 10:1–12. His steps are very easy to follow: go to a town, offer peace, see if anyone offers you hospitality, eat what they give you, share the good news of the kingdom, and offer to pray for healing. The simplicity of the steps offers a steady guiding hand, helping people know how to proceed even though they have no idea what the outcome will be. What will happen is unknown, but the steps themselves are clear. This is essential for designing an action learning experiment.

Third, the final part is creating a feedback loop. This is an opportunity for the people who tried the experiment to discuss what happened and what they learned. This is crucial because the feedback loop is where you actually gather the learning that was gained by trying the experiment. If you don't make time for reflection and discussion, the point of the experiment is lost. Remember, the main purpose of action learning experiments is the learning and transformation

## Action Learning Experiments

Define what you
want to learn

Name your
action steps

Create a
feedback loop

of the people who participate in them. In the absence of reflection, people who participated don't get the opportunity to recognize all that they learned through the experiment.

## Designing an Experiment

Here is an example of an action learning experiment Michael tried with a church he helped start in an urban neighborhood. The experiment evolved from the congregation's listening work. A group of people were doing a Prayer Walk in the neighborhood around the school where the church met for Sunday worship. During their walk, they noticed several big purple buses stopping to pick people up. The buses were labeled with the name of a casino that was forty-five minutes away from the neighborhood. Seeing the buses prompted curiosity in the group, and they discovered that the buses made several stops each day in the neighborhood, offering free rides to anyone who wanted to go to the casino. As they processed what they had learned, they were inspired to ask the following question: *How is God already present in the lives of our neighbors who ride the casino bus?* Their listening led the group to design an action learning experiment to help them find out more about how God might be engaged in the lives of these neighbors.

How should the team of people approach their neighbors who are riding the purple casino bus in order to discover how God is present in their lives? Designing an action learning experiment that engages others requires careful consideration and respect for those you would like to engage. We want to design experiments where we can be transparent about our intentions. We don't want to force people to interact with us or create a "bait and switch" experience for people who might be hesitant about getting involved with Christians. But we also don't want to shy away from reaching our neighbors out of fear that they won't want to talk with us. Like Paul and his companions, we have the life-changing news of Jesus, and it matters that we seek opportunities to build relationships with people.

The church team came up with the following steps for engaging the people on the purple casino bus. Pairs of people would get on the bus at different stops. They would sit near people and try to start a conversation. If the bus riders weren't interested in talking, the people from the congregation wouldn't keep pressing. When asked why they were on the bus, the people from the church said they were part of a local congregation that was interested in hearing the stories of their neighbors who used the bus service. They weren't there to recruit anyone to come to church or even to share their faith. The point of the experiment was just to get to know the people who rode the bus and to hear their stories if they wanted to share them. The teams would ride the bus down to the casino, get off, eat dinner together at the buffet, and share stories about their experiences of riding the bus. The sharing formed the feedback loop to process what happened.

Michael remembered getting on the bus with a friend and thinking, *This is one of the worst ideas we've ever come up with!* He is not someone who enjoys meeting strangers, and the idea of connecting with people he didn't know was very intimidating. *What if someone didn't want to talk?* He felt very vulnerable and outside his comfort zone as they started.

We imagine this might have been how Paul and his companions felt as they entered yet another town wondering if they would find warm hospitality on their journey. But their dependence upon God is something that would richly benefit our congregations today. We must be willing to put ourselves in situations where we depend on the hospitality and reception of others. This is very different from always asking people to enter our spaces and receive our hospitality. How often do we consider the vulnerability of our neighbors as we ask them to step outside their comfort zones and enter our worship space?

Each member of the church team got on the bus and talked with people who were traveling to the casino. The responses were mixed. Some people were happy to talk. Others made it clear they weren't interested in conversation. As the team members dined later at the casino buffet, they listened to one another share their experiences, how they felt, and what they thought God might be teaching them about their neighbors. Several of the pairs had profound conversations with people on the bus who shared deep experiences from their lives. Others had more surface-level conversations. Some didn't talk at all. But as they processed the experience, they realized how much they had learned no matter how the conversations went. One discovery was that there were a lot of people in their neighborhood who were open to conversation and new relationships. Many of the people were not likely going to come to a worship service. But by placing themselves in a space where the people already were—where they already felt comfortable—the congregation had the opportunity to build relationships, receive hospitality, and learn about their neighbors' lives.

As you read this story, you might be thinking that it's slightly insane to get on a purple casino bus to try to meet people. It is true that this was a pretty challenging action learning experiment. Your experiments can be less complex and require a bit less vulnerability. We have a collection of examples of other action learning experiments on the Faith+Lead website to help you get started. Go to the Resources for the Journey section at the end of the book to learn more.

You might begin with something simple, like borrowing a tool or an ingredient from your neighbor or asking someone to teach you about something they have expertise in. Even small experiments can still help us learn how to engage with people outside our congregations in ways that build mutual relationships and trust.

## Leading People into Action

Leading people to try these kinds of action learning experiments can be challenging. Most people do not like to do things they haven't done before. People get uncomfortable when they aren't sure what the end result is going to be. This is why it's vital to create an environment where people feel safe enough to try new things together. The leader must cheer people on as their capacity for this work increases. When people begin to try new things, they need to be celebrated and affirmed no matter how it turns out. That's why the role of the ministry leader is essential in this journey. In faithful innovation, the pastor serves as a spiritual guide and encourager—someone who helps the other participants find the courage to try things that put them outside of their comfort zones.

One of the keys to effectively leading the Act step in the faithful innovation journey is to design action learning experiments that are simple, repeatable, and affordable. Your experiments should not be wildly disruptive to the life of your church. They should begin at the periphery of congregational life rather than at its center. We encourage people to start with actions that won't threaten the things people care deeply about. For example, instead of experimenting with a new liturgy or worship element, encourage a team of people to simply spend time in their community and notice where they see God's presence outside the walls of the church. If you design an action learning experiment that is very expensive and changes something that matters greatly to people, you will meet with strong resistance right away. You might have a hard time building momentum for the rest of the faithful innovation journey.

Here's an example of a very simple action learning experiment. One of our congregations wanted to learn how to build relationships with their neighbors. They recognized that adult friendships don't happen automatically just because people live near one another. In fact, many people go to and from their apartments or homes without ever engaging with their neighbors. The church wanted to tackle this problem, so they designed a simple, low-cost action learning experiment to help them discover how to help people bridge this gap in connection.

The experiment required an investment in some plastic Adirondack chairs. These are widely available from the local thrift shops or home-improvement stores. Members of the congregation put pairs of these chairs out in front of their own homes and committed to spending time sitting in the chairs each day. This was admittedly an odd thing to do. In this church's context, people usually sat outside in the back of their homes or apartments where there was more privacy. By intentionally being present in the front yard almost every day for thirty minutes, the members of the church began to engage

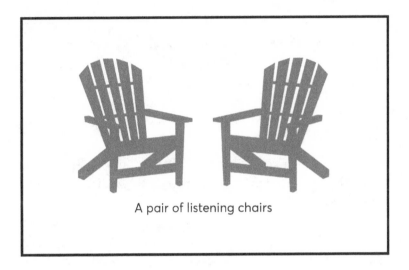

A pair of listening chairs

their neighbors differently. People walking their dogs would stop and say hello. The people from the church started to notice kids playing in their neighborhoods. Some neighbors came out of their own houses after a few weeks to introduce themselves. They said they had seen people sitting in front of their houses and had been meaning to come over and get acquainted. The simplicity of this experiment contributed to its outcome. It didn't need complex planning or scheduling, because people were at home already. It just required the participants to behave differently and pay attention to what they learned. They started to see some of what God was doing in the lives of their neighbors just by sitting in lawn chairs.

Ministry leaders can help people in their congregations try experiments like this one. The people in our churches should be encouraged to attempt things that build upon their listening work and that cost them only their time and vulnerability. Engaging in the faithful innovation journey doesn't have to be expensive. It doesn't have to be expansive either. The best action learning experiments are simple, repeatable, and affordable. All they ask is that we take risks to connect with those around us in new ways. They invite us to enter into spaces where we don't have control so we can learn to see how God might be present there.

## Lessons from Failure

It is essential for church leaders to foster an environment where it is OK for the experiment to "fail." Most people think of failure in terms of the outcome of whatever they are trying. They might believe an action learning experiment is a failure if the people they engage with don't respond in the way they hoped or expected. But the "success" of an experiment is better understood in terms of the learning value it creates for the people who participated. The most important thing that comes out of an action learning experiment is our own learning. Action learning experiments are about trying something new in order to learn how to be the church in the twenty-first century. The only real way an experiment can fail is if we don't try and we don't learn. Ministry leaders must emphasize this point repeatedly when they are helping people take the Act step in the faithful innovation process. As long as we make the effort and learn something, we cannot fail. What we learn is what helps us know the next step to take, which is what faithful innovation is all about.

> " The most important thing that comes out of an action learning experiment is our own learning. "

Moreover, we actually have little control over the outcome of our experiments. As we prayerfully involve God in both our plans and implementation, we will see that it is God who orchestrates the results rather than our own efforts. A key component of innovating faithfully is trusting God to do the work, whether that is to bring about a specific change, reveal something important, or simply take us and the people in our communities one step further on the journey of discipleship and spiritual formation. We are invited to watch carefully for the Spirit's movement in and through our experiments regardless of what happens.

It is also crucial that we pay close attention to the impact we might be having on those around us as we begin our experiments. The last thing we would want to do is to harm our neighbors as we seek to learn how to love them. We want to design ways to learn about how God is active in our contexts without doing harm to anyone. As Jesus moved about from place to place, he always respected the people he encountered, even if he challenged them and invited them to follow him. We must be committed to doing the same as we seek to discover how to join what God is doing in our neighborhoods.

Ministry leaders can cultivate a supportive environment by talking about their own anxieties as they try new things. Sharing with others how doing an experiment makes us feel can help normalize the anxiety that comes with trying and learning new things. Pastors and church leaders can be particularly helpful in this regard; when they share that they get nervous when they engage with people in new ways, it helps their congregations feel less concerned about their own fears. This is why it is so important for leaders to try the experiments alongside the members of their congregations. Leaders are full participants in the Listen-Act-Share journey. Working through the process together builds people's courage to keep trying even when they are uncomfortable.

## Steps for Getting Started

At this point, you might be wondering how you can begin leading an action learning experiment with people in your church. We've compiled the following steps to help get you started:

- Invite a small group of people to join a team focused on practicing faithful innovation. Use whatever language for the team that makes the most sense in your context: experiment team, guiding team, R&D ministry team, faithful innovation team, and so on.
- Help your team pay attention to God by utilizing the listening practices in the previous chapter: Dwelling in the Word, Spiritual Journey Conversations, and Prayer Walks.
- Design an experiment with your team that will help you learn about some aspects of your listening work. If your team heard about how people are struggling with mental health challenges, for example, you might design an action learning experiment that focuses on that topic.
- Make sure your action learning experiment has three things: a carefully defined learning objective, clear action steps, and a feedback loop where you can discuss what you learned.
- Organize a time for the team to try your action learning experiment together. If you can't do it with the entire team, have at least two people try it together.
- Schedule a meeting time when the entire team can share together what they did and learned. Much of the learning comes from reflecting on their actions, asking questions that help the team interpret what they did and what it means.

- Develop a plan to share stories of your experiences with people outside of the team. This can happen on Sundays at worship, through newsletters, on the website, or through social media.

## Becoming a New Kind of Church

The primary goal of the faithful innovation journey is to learn or relearn how to follow the leading of the Holy Spirit together as a congregation. Faithful innovation isn't just about trying new things. It is about building the capacity to learn how God might be inviting a congregation to live as the church in new ways. That's why faithful innovation is a journey or a process and not a program. It is a cycle of listening, acting, and sharing that helps us continuously seek and pay attention to God's leading, step out in faith based on what we hear, and tell others about our experiences. This is a way of life rather than a plan to address specific problems the congregation might be facing right now. Yet it is possible for the people of the church to design an experiment that promotes learning while simultaneously speaking to the needs of their particular context.

> " *The primary goal of the faithful innovation journey is to learn or relearn how to follow the leading of the Holy Spirit together as a congregation.* "

A congregation in rural Wisconsin wondered how they might play a role in honoring and encouraging local farmers. On their neighborhood "walks," which were actually drives through the area, they recognized anew how much farming defined their community. They designed an action learning experiment to help them discover how to thank the farmers for their work. They decided to make meals for the farmers, assembling small brown-bag lunches with cards that read, "Thank you for feeding the world." Once the lunches were prepared, the team drove out to the grain elevators and to the fields to deliver them. They offered prayers to the workers and to their loved ones, proclaiming thanksgiving for the food God had provided to the rest of the community through their work. Many of the farmers who encountered the people from the congregation deeply appreciated that they took the time to honor their work and offer their prayers. Some even invited the church members to return in the spring to pray over their fields at planting time.

## Challenges of the Act Step

One of the most challenging parts of the Act step in the faithful innovation journey is answering the *why* question. Once your congregation participates in listening work and moves ahead to trying some action learning experiments, people are going to ask why you are experimenting and what you hope to gain. They might wonder, *Are these experiments going to help invite more people to worship? Are these experiments going to help us get more young people into our church?* These are legitimate questions you will need to address at this point in the process.

Here is a succinct answer to the *why are we doing this* question. We do action learning experiments to learn new ways to be the church and to be transformed personally as followers of Jesus. These experiments are less about the people we're reaching and more about opportunities for the congregation to grow as disciples of Jesus. Christian discipleship is fundamental to the mission of the

church, and we grow in Christ-likeness when we put ourselves in vulnerable positions, humbly engaging our neighbors as we learn to love
them well.

> " We do action learning experiments to learn new ways to be the
> church and to be transformed personally as followers of Jesus. "

If we want to learn how to be the church in the twenty-first
century, *we* must change. We have to be transformed. We cannot
externalize or outsource the change that needs to happen in many
congregations. We can't become the kind of church we want to be
only by hiring a new pastor, changing our worship style, improving
our website, or raising more money. The change has to begin with
all of us. We have to become people who know how to get outside
our comfort zones and connect with our neighbors in ways that build
trust and mutual respect.

This trust will give us the chance to notice ways the Spirit of
God is already at work in the lives of those around us, and it will clarify how our congregations can join in the work that God is doing in
and through our neighbors. This is a totally different approach from
assuming that our job is to invite people to meet God through joining our own church activities (like worship, small groups, or serving).
We are talking about a paradigm shift in our perception and understanding of what the primary activities of the church should be.

## What Experiments Are and Aren't

We've given you a lot to digest about experiments. Because clarity
matters when it comes to experiments, we want to make sure you are

clear on what an experiment is and what it isn't. Here's a list to help further refine your understanding.

**What makes for a good experiment:**

- starts with a simple action
- doesn't cost a lot of money
- incorporates learnings from our listening work
- has a clear learning goal
- has very clear steps on how to do it

Good experiments often require taking a relational risk in engaging the people around us. This helps us get outside our comfort zones and often takes us outside the walls of our churches. These experimental actions may include steps that help us learn how to receive hospitality from others, which is what Jesus often did.

It's important that our experiments are designed so a wide variety of people can participate in them if they choose. Experiments invite participants to try something new together, even if they don't know what the result of these new actions will be. Failure is OK as long as participants learn from what they try. Good experiments begin "on the side" in a congregation—they don't disrupt the primary activities, like Sunday worship, that people value most.

**What doesn't make for a good experiment:**

- steps are too complicated
- requires too much money to do
- no clear learning objective
- outcome is already determined
- no one is willing to try it

If an experiment isn't something a lot of people can try or seems too risky, it won't be as effective. Helpful experiments are open-ended and learning oriented, while less helpful experiments might merely be potential programs that people want to launch. If an experiment ignores God's role and focuses primarily on human effort and activity, it won't create the kind of learning we're hoping for.

The challenge of engaging in action learning experiments is that they don't always immediately result in improved metrics like greater worship attendance or giving in a local congregation. This is a hard reality, and it can make some people wonder if experiments are really worth doing. People might respond by saying that ministry isn't about attendance and giving, so we shouldn't worry about those things. While this is true to an extent, it is also true that we want more people to worship God with us, to come to know Jesus, and to join our congregation in participating in God's work in the world. The faithful innovation journey is a way to help us experience personal transformation so we become a different kind of church. In order for our church to change, we personally and collectively have to change first. Action learning experiments often don't directly impact things like attendance and giving. But they *do* impact the kind of disciples we are becoming, and this makes us the kind of church that other people do want to join.

## The Prayers of Lydia

We worked with a group of congregations in upstate New York who wondered how God might be leading them to engage with their neighbors. This "God question" led them to try an action learning experiment that would allow them to learn more about the struggles and yearnings of their neighbors. We introduced them to an experiment known as "prayer flags" that had been piloted by a church in Tennessee.

The action steps were straightforward. The congregation identified a public event in their community (like a farmer's market,
summer festival, or outdoor social gathering). They approached the
event organizers and asked for permission to set up a table where
they would invite people to share prayer requests. Small strips of
cloth were available for people to write down their prayer requests if
they wanted, or they could pray right then with members of the
church. The requests could also be anonymous. The written prayer
flags were then tied to a display during the event, and all of the
prayer requests were eventually collected and brought back to
the congregation. A team of people read them and prayed for them
at the church. The congregation implemented a feedback loop by
reflecting on what they learned from collecting the prayer requests.

People who planned to do this prayer flag experiment were
often nervous about it. They wrestled with concerns like, *What if
they couldn't get permission to put up a table at their local event? What
if no one stopped to share a prayer request? What if people did stop
and wanted someone to pray with them out loud?* There were a lot of
unknowns in terms of how this experiment might play out. But every
aspect of the experiment was clear, from the learning goal to the
steps to the feedback loop.

The churches in upstate New York conducted the experiment
over the course of one summer, and the response was very surprising.
Hundreds of people stopped at these prayer flag booths at the different events and offered their prayer requests. Some people chose
to pray right at the booths, and others left their prayer requests for
others to pray for. Some churches that have done this experiment
have decided to transform the prayer flags they received into altar
cloths so that they celebrate the Eucharist over the prayers of their
neighbors during worship. Many congregations were overwhelmed
by the volume of requests that came in. This experiment gave these

churches a deeper understanding of the needs expressed by their neighbors and their desire for God to respond to those needs. These were the prayer requests of the Lydias in each church's community. The congregations found neighbors who were seeking God, and most of them were not already attending a local church.

## A New Question

The outcome of the prayer flag experiment was so positive that some people wanted to offer prayer flag booths all over the state the following year. While that might have been a great idea, there was a deeper spiritual question God seemed to be inviting the congregations to wrestle with as a result of the experiment: *How might God want to offer healing to our neighbors who have shared some of their deepest struggles and hurts with us?* This launched a whole new cycle of listening and acting focused on discovering how God might work through these congregations to offer healing to both their neighbors and themselves. The feedback loop created space for reflection that didn't lead to repeating the same experiment over and over again. Instead, it built upon the learning from that experiment and led to entirely new experimental actions.

The faithful innovation journey is continuous—congregations don't ever "arrive" at the end of the process. We keep learning how to innovate faithfully as we follow God's leading throughout our lives. This journey is not one that tries to "fix" your church or ensure stability or security for the next generation. It is a journey designed to help us continually grow and change. Learning to behave your way into new thinking requires a lot of vulnerability and courage in a local congregation. Convincing people to try new ways of being the church that place people outside their comfort zones can be a big challenge. But once a group experiences the learning and personal transformation that come from experimentation, energy blossoms within the congregation. The stories that these experimenters share with others in the church allow the faithful innovation journey to impact the entire congregation, not just the people who participate directly. Sharing our stories of learning and transformation makes it possible for others in the church to learn and change too. In the next chapter, we will see how sharing these stories invites others to take the faithful innovation journey.

# Four

## Share

Riley was sure that something strange was happening at church. All month long, a small group had been meeting together and going out on weeknights to do some sort of "experiments" with people in the community. One of Riley's friends was on the team, and he kept talking about meeting with some of the neighbors around the church building to have conversations about where they saw God at work in their lives. Riley's friend had been so amazed about how cool the work was and about the powerful questions and comments the team kept getting from people outside the church. Riley was skeptical. She wasn't sure the church should be focused on the neighborhood. She thought about the needs of the church members. Wasn't there already enough work to do right here? Aren't the people who belong to the church the ones who we should be concentrating on? But a part of her was intrigued by the stories she was hearing. Maybe there was something to these experiments after all. Riley decided she needed to find out more from her friend after worship on Sunday.

_____

How might an entire congregation begin to take this faithful innovation journey together? Many change efforts in all kinds of industries and social settings begin with a small percentage of people trying new things and adopting new behaviors, with the majority of people joining the movement later. This is true in the church, too, as initial teams learn new ways to be the church in their context without the rest of the congregation. But if the transformative change is only experienced by a few people, then the rest of the congregation won't shift. As churches and their leaders begin this journey, they often ask, *How do we get more people on board with this work?* The simplest answer to this question is, *By sharing your stories!* The next step of the faithful innovation journey is Share. This chapter will walk through how sharing stories about what you learn from your action learning experiments can inspire others to join you in the work.

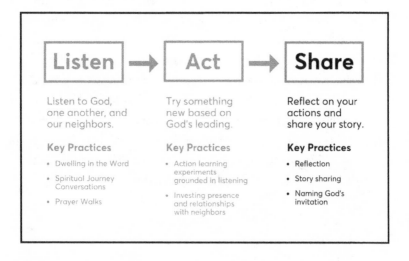

| Listen | Act | Share |
|--------|-----|-------|
| Listen to God, one another, and our neighbors. | Try something new based on God's leading. | Reflect on your actions and share your story. |
| **Key Practices** | **Key Practices** | **Key Practices** |
| • Dwelling in the Word | • Action learning experiments grounded in listening | • Reflection |
| • Spiritual Journey Conversations | • Investing presence and relationships with neighbors | • Story sharing |
| • Prayer Walks | | • Naming God's invitation |

## Sharing the Story of Lydia

The early Christian church experienced some significant internal disagreements as the good news of Jesus began to spread to people outside the Jewish community. Paul and other disciples traveled to places outside of Israel to tell people about who Jesus was and what he did. This caused gentiles to want to become followers of Jesus. Paul and his companions saw how the Holy Spirit was present in the lives of these people who chose to follow Jesus. They returned to Jerusalem and shared the stories of how God was at work in people around the world.

The first Christians were Jewish converts, and so the members of the early church debated if and how these new gentile believers should be included in their community. This challenged some previous beliefs that the Israelites were the only people who could be included in God's family. Acts 15 includes the debate on this issue among various groups. Paul shared stories about how he and his companions had seen the Spirit of God working through believers who had non-Jewish backgrounds. He told about people being healed, speaking in tongues, and after accepting Paul's message, turning and sharing the good news of Jesus with others. These stories demonstrated how God was already at work among the gentiles, and it had a huge influence on the decision of the Jerusalem Council to include these new believers as full members of the early church. Stories about God working in the world have power, and this early example of spiritual storytelling proves just how far-reaching they can be.

The journey that brought Paul and his companions to Lydia in the very next chapter in Acts (Acts 16) comes right after the Jerusalem Council's decision. The story of Lydia's conversion to the Christian faith and her persuasion of Paul and his companions to come stay at her house would be shared far beyond Macedonia. Lydia became known for several "firsts": she was the first European convert to Christianity, and she was the founder of the first church in Philippi.[1] Lydia became an influential leader who inspired other female leaders in the church for generations to come.

The book of Acts, recorded by Luke, is largely a collection of stories about how the Spirit of God worked in and through the Christians of the early church. These stories were included in what we now call the New Testament in the Bible in part because they were so widely used by the early church as sacred texts. The development of the scriptural canon is itself a testimony to the power and influence of telling God's stories.

## Faithfully Innovative Sharing

The third step in the faithful innovation journey is Share. This step is focused on sharing the stories from the experiences of those who are listening and trying action learning experiments. These stories need to be shared on a regular basis with the whole congregation as well as with people outside the congregation. Telling these stories is about celebrating what God is doing and also about inviting other people to join in the work. This step is essential for building momentum and helping foster transformative change across the entire congregation.

Reflecting on what has been done and what has been learned is a powerful step that helps clarify how God might be leading a congregation forward. Reflection is perhaps the most difficult part of the journey because it can be easily overlooked—people can quickly move on from one experiment to the next without ever pausing to consider what they're learning. Yet stopping for reflection is how the congregation becomes awakened to its own growth and development. Regular reflection should become part of the rhythms of a congregation's life. Without it, the first two steps (Listen and Act) will be little more than temporary moments of trying something before moving on to something else. Once you have completed your experiments, it is important to reflect on what you have learned. It is through your reflections that you will uncover what your next actions might be.

Reflection involves asking, *What did you do? What happened? What did you learn?* The last question can include three additional parts: what you learned from your failures, where you discovered new energy, and how God might be inviting you and your congregation into the neighborhood.

Inviting people to reflect on what they learned is the core of this story-sharing step. Remember, action learning experiments are primarily designed to help the participants *learn* something and experience transformation themselves. Part of the reflection practice is considering what you learned from your "failures"—from the things that didn't go well or didn't go how you expected. Failure is a normal part of learning and trying new things. It's important that people understand this as they reflect on what they tried through their experiments. The only real failures in action learning experiments come from lack of trying and lack of learning. No matter how the experiment turns out, something can be learned. But many participants in the faithful innovation journey feel like they failed somehow. They are conditioned to see success in narrow terms. Church leaders can help by destigmatizing or normalizing failure, inviting the congregation to think about it together and name the learning that might come from the feeling of failure. Questions like *Has anything you tried felt like it has failed so far?* or *What did it look like?* or *What did you learn from that?* can help a group process perceived failures and capture learning. These practices of reflection and story sharing help people move beyond feeling unsettled when things don't go as they planned or as they hoped. Learning is always possible in *every* situation, and it's especially valuable when it helps us change course to a new direction.

> " The only real failures in action learning experiments come from lack of trying and lack of learning. "

Many people report that they feel a new kind of energy as they engage in the faithful innovation journey. People get energized as they begin to experience a new way of being the church together. The energy is palpable in a room full of people sharing stories about what they did in their action learning experiments. These are not just stories of human activity—they are stories of God's activity through human agents. Partnering with God in a new way often results in a release of new energy both inside and outside of the congregation. We believe this energy is created by God's Spirit; it's a tangible expression of God's presence in the midst of this journey.

The practice of story sharing can create an opportunity for participants to reflect on where they experienced God's energy. Naming this new energy motivates people to share what they have learned with others and to keep engaging in listening and action learning because they can feel the difference it is already making in their community.

> The practice of story sharing invites reflection on where God was present in the experiments using these prompts: *Did your experiment seem to generate some new energy with your guiding team, the participants in your experiment, or both? Why do you think there was new energy?*

Processing the learning from listening and from action learning experiments also involves naming how God might be inviting the congregation to move forward. As we behave our way into new thinking, we begin to see a picture of the future God might have in mind for our congregation. Church leaders can help their people begin to wonder about what vision God might have for them and where God might be inviting them to go next.

> The practice of naming God's invitation includes these questions: *How might God be inviting you into partnership with God's work in the neighborhood? What clues could be pointing you in a new direction?*

## Asking God Questions of Your Stories

Many people wonder what's next after doing some listening and action learning. We acknowledge that it can be difficult to determine what the next step should be. The key to discovering the path forward is learning to ask "God questions" about the work we have done so far. While it may be helpful to do more listening, more experimenting, and more story sharing, the ultimate goal for the faithful innovation journey is determining how God might be inviting you to partner with the work God is already doing. Here are a few examples of "God questions" you can ask of your work so far:

- As you listened to other people, in what ways did they say God had impacted their lives (i.e., through relationships, experiences, Scripture, church activities, etc.)?
- As you paid attention to your neighborhood, in what ways did you notice God was present or active?
- As you listened to Scripture together, what themes or insights did God bring about in your conversations?
- As you shared your stories about your action learning experiments, where did God bring new energy to your team and your congregation?
- As you engaged in your action learning experiments, did you notice any ways people were hurting or suffering? How do you think God wants to respond to that hurting or suffering? How might you join God in that response?
- When you listen to the stories of others who engaged in an action learning experiment, do you see any themes that God may want you to pay attention to? Or is there one key story that God is using to really grab your heart?

> " The ultimate goal for the faithful innovation journey is determining how God might be inviting you to partner with the work God is already doing. "

Engaging these kinds of "God questions" can help clarify the *Now what?* question that many people ask after they've taken the steps in the faithful innovation journey for the first time.

What might God be leading your congregation to try next? Reflection and story sharing can sometimes reveal the next steps for a congregation. We worked with a group of churches in Ohio that spent multiple years engaging the faithful innovation process together. They did a lot of listening work and tried all kinds of action learning experiments. When they shared their stories and reflected on what they had done, they saw three different themes emerge from their work together. The themes—engage with God around issues of local justice, learn to help start new congregations, and find new ways to talk about the gospel with people outside of the church—seemed like ways God was inviting them to focus their energy going forward. This clarity allowed them to start exploring what resources they might need and what changes they should make to start pursuing these areas.

Congregations can engage in reflection by asking, *What new questions do we have now? What should we do next? How can we share what we're learning? How might God be leading us to move forward in light of what we've learned through this journey?*

## Helping People Share Their Stories

There are some simple ways to put the story-sharing step into practice. First, *it is important to teach people how to share their stories.* Many people get anxious about sharing a story publicly. Giving people a simple outline for what to say helps them to prepare to share their stories. Often, people who are engaged in faithful innovation are more comfortable describing what *they* did and what *they* learned rather than describing God's activity. Asking them to reflect and share about where they may have sensed God's presence in their listening or action learning experiment can be more difficult. It is essential to practice naming where we see God's involvement in our lives so that we become more comfortable recognizing God's presence among us.

> To help people share their stories, give them a simple outline that asks them to describe what they did, talk about what they learned, and share if there was any way they sensed God's presence in what they tried.

We recently experimented with hosting a story-sharing event at a local brewery. The theme of the event was "stories of home." We scheduled an evening gathering and invited both church people and people who regularly frequented the brewery. We let people know they would have the chance to share a story of what "home" meant to them. Some people loved the chance to stand up in front of a group of people and share a story! Others were eager to participate but were uncomfortable standing up in front of people. So we created a second option for them—we let them write a summary of their story on a piece of paper that someone else would read aloud. About half of the people who wanted to share chose the written option.

Telling our stories is a vulnerable activity. Leaders must create spaces where people can safely experiment. The same is true for storytelling. Leaders are responsible for cultivating an environment where people can share their stories. We've seen this done well in a variety of ways. A natural opportunity for people to share stories is to gather them together after they have tried an action learning experiment. This can happen either in person or online, and the purpose of the gathering is simply to tell stories and discuss the learning from the experiment.

Another possibility is to reserve a regular part of each worship service for the practice of sharing stories. Some congregations have a monthly rhythm of taking three to five minutes to share stories about what people are learning from their participation in the faithful innovation process. This practice can also expand to include stories of how God is at work in the lives of people in the congregation. When others hear these stories, they become better equipped to see God in daily life and also enabled to join God in God's work in the world. Opening space in the worship liturgy for this kind of story sharing ignites the energy of the congregation and helps people see the value and purpose of the faithful innovation process.

If you want to share to a wider audience, you might consider recording short videos or writing brief summaries about what your team is learning through the listening work and action learning experiments. These pieces can be shared with people outside the congregation through websites, social media, or other distribution channels. Sharing stories in these ways invites a new set of important questions:

- How do we explain what we are trying and learning in words that anyone could understand, even if they are not part of our congregation?
- If these videos or written pieces get shared broadly online, is there an opportunity for people to join us in this work?

These are difficult questions for congregations that are primarily used to communicating with one another using shared language that everyone inside the church understands. The reality is that there are people outside the church who are searching for God and who want to find a community of supportive people to help them grow spiritually. These Lydias might see a video or a written post online and want to engage with the kind of church that would spend time listening to the spiritual stories of strangers. Would your church be ready if Lydia arrived on your doorstep? What would you say to her? How would you welcome her?

Studies have shown that many people are very open to exploring spirituality and faith.[2] Public story sharing provides an avenue within the faithful innovation journey that can open your church to greater visibility and connections with neighbors. In a world shaped by the Covid-19 pandemic, the Lydias of the world are more likely to check out your congregation online before ever visiting in person. Many people want to be part of a congregation that tries new things, that intentionally listens to other people in order to learn from them, and that offers authentic and adaptable spiritual community. Public story sharing is like creating a window into the life of your congregation, offering views that would otherwise be nearly impossible to see. We believe that the public sharing of congregational stories is one significant way God intends for people to be welcomed into God's kingdom in the twenty-first century.

> " We believe that the public sharing of congregational stories is one significant way God intends for people to be welcomed into God's kingdom in the twenty-first century. "

The Share step in the faithful innovation journey is what helps to create the conditions for change in your congregation. There needs to be a sense of urgency about sharing these stories of what God is doing through these action learning experiments and about what God is doing in the everyday lives of your people. It is the sharing of stories that deepens the congregation's understanding of how God is leading. It is through story sharing that other people—beyond those who are directly engaged in the listening and action learning—can hear about what's happening and feel a sense of ownership and participation in the journey. Sharing stories is what builds momentum for change within a congregation. It is what fans the flame of God's Spirit. It invites transformation in the lives of a broad range of people. The practice of sharing stories is how people hear about the amazing ways God is present and active in the life of a congregation.

## Challenges of the Share Step

Churches that begin this journey of faithful innovation often reach a point where they are wondering about how to get more people involved. Usually, a small team of people in a congregation will initially do the listening and experimental work described in the last two chapters. As few as five to ten people will take those steps, and they will personally start to see the ways God is inviting the congregation as a whole to engage differently with their neighbors and their community. Those same five to ten people will often have a lot of energy and enthusiasm for continuing to listen and try new things, but they will begin to wonder how they might get others to join and how they might spread their excitement. They quickly realize that if they don't get other people involved, the journey will only impact them and will not have an influence on the congregation as a whole. So they rightfully ask, *How can we get more people to join us on this faithful innovation journey?* This is an essential question for anyone interested in bringing transformation to an entire congregation. One of the biggest challenges of this step is figuring out how to share stories with a broad range of people so they can be impacted by the learning process even if they haven't participated in it directly themselves.

Many people think they must get 100 percent of people— everyone—to accept an innovation in order for it to be adopted into their congregation. This isn't true. Studies on leading change in organizations suggest that if just 20 percent of a group begins to adopt a new way of doing things, that innovation has a good chance of being accepted by the whole group over time.[3] This means that if an innovation can gain early support among just a few people, it has a good chance of becoming part of the life of the congregation over the long term.

Sharing stories about the listening work and the action learning experiments is one way to help people join the work and adopt an innovation in a congregation. Stories help people who are more resistant to change see the tangible impact these new ways of doing things are having on people like them in the congregation. When someone who is hesitant hears a story shared by someone at a Sunday worship service about how they listened to people's spiritual stories in a local pub, for example, that person might begin to realize what a big impact the work could have on their life and the lives of others. They may even want to try some of these new ways of doing things themselves or at least show their support for those who are trying them.

Here's an example of the kind of story we're talking about. A small team of people from a Presbyterian congregation gathered in a local pub. They planned to see if anyone in the pub wanted to share a story about their own spiritual journey. As they looked at one another around the high-top table, no one felt like they could actually ask someone in the pub to share. One brave member of the team volunteered to try first. He crossed the room, introduced himself, and started a conversation. After authentically sharing that a group from his church had come to listen to people's stories, almost everyone in the pub engaged with the team and shared about their spiritual journeys. The team left that evening amazed at the openness of the people in the pub and their willingness to share.

The participants in this experiment later shared the story of their pub experience at a training event for congregations in their regional denomination. Their story impacted the ministry leaders in that room in a profound way. The leaders' imaginations were transformed for how they might engage with people in their own local communities. There was a sense among the leaders that maybe there were more people in neighborhoods and workplaces who would be interested in sharing their own spiritual backgrounds. The stories created hope that there might be greater interest in talking about spiritual things than they had assumed. The courage of the people who tried out this action learning experiment inspired people in other congregations to try their own experiments. The original act of storytelling multiplied until it influenced far more people than those at the brewery.

This is the power of a story to help other people participate in the faithful innovation journey, and it is a power that operates on multiple levels. First, the practice of sharing a story helps the storyteller reflect on what they learned and how they have grown. This helps solidify the learning they've gained so they can continue to build upon it. Second, the stories help other people see what a difference the faithful innovation journey can make in the lives of people just like them. Sharing stories helps build momentum in the congregation as more people see the benefit of change. Third, these stories are a great way for people from the local community to get to know what is happening in the congregation. The stories open a window into the life of the congregation for those who might be interested in learning more about the church and the difference Jesus makes in the lives of those who are part of it.

Sharing stories regularly can help reshape the very culture and makeup of a congregation. Beginning to reimagine what life in that kind of congregation might be like is where we will turn in the next chapter.

# Five

# Faithful Innovation as a Way of Life for the Church

First Church had been engaging in the practices of Listen-Act-Share, led by a small team that had been experimenting with forming relationships through a local community garden. Working plots alongside their neighbors had led to conversations, which had led eventually to shared meals and the exchanging of hospitality in restaurants and homes. Many of these conversations had entered into spiritual territory, and congregation members had become comfortable asking neighbors about their spiritual journeys, sharing their own faith stories, and offering prayer. As more people from the church became involved in these practices, they began to question the old patterns of committees, programs, and internal activities at First Church that weren't nearly as energizing anymore. They wondered how their church could focus more on these life-giving relationships with neighbors instead.

———————————

Juanita had grown increasingly frustrated with the established church. The congregations in her area seemed focused on institutional agendas that were disconnected from what she and her young friends cared about. Those churches weren't asking or answering their questions about faith and life. Her pastor recognized this and began to encourage Juanita to experiment with starting a new expression of church within her group of spiritually curious but religiously unaffiliated friends. This new kind of church would begin meeting where these friends were already gathering—at a local coffee shop—and it would center on simple practices of spiritual storytelling, imaginative engagement of biblical texts, prayer, mutual support, and service toward neighbors. Juanita was excited about this prospect but wondered how she should get started.

We all begin the faithful innovation journey from different starting points. You may be reading this book as a leader or as a member of an existing congregation that is seeking to deepen its connections with God and its neighbors. You may be curious about how to discover new vitality among those already gathered in the church as well as how to build meaningful connections with people in the community outside the church. Or you may already have left the inherited church, finding it inhospitable to you and your calling as a follower of Jesus. Rather than working to transform an existing congregation, you may wonder how to participate in cultivating new forms of Christian community that will connect authentically with people you know who are far from church and skeptical about organized religion.

This chapter will explore how the faithful innovation journey is a way of life, both for existing congregations and for new Christian communities the Holy Spirit seeks to birth in our time. Faithful innovation is not just another program or occasional activity done to "fix" a church problem. It is a set of practices that become habits and transform how we as the church approach the challenges and opportunities facing us. It involves unlearning old defaults as we discover new and life-giving ways forward. It invites us into an expanded imagination of what church might look like in order to connect faithfully with the Lydias—our spiritually curious neighbors—in our communities, cities, and neighborhoods.

## Beginning from Within

The early Christian apostles usually began their engagement in a new town or city by starting at the local synagogue. Christianity emerged from within first-century Judaism, and the synagogue was the natural starting place to share the good news about Jesus. Paul himself had been extensively trained in Jewish teaching and custom; he could relate culturally and theologically with the people in the synagogues. In other words, Paul could speak their language on multiple levels. Paul understood what God was doing in Jesus—this was not a cancellation of God's work among the Jews but an extension of the promises God made to Israel. Those promises were now for all people, including those who were not culturally or religiously Jewish. Through Jesus, the gentiles were being grafted like a wild branch onto the original olive tree of Israel (Rom 11:1–32). God's faithfulness to Israel endures but is also revealed to be far more expansive than people realized, encompassing those disconnected by heritage, practice, and culture from Judaism.

If you're beginning the faithful innovation journey from within an existing local church, this analogy is fruitful to keep in mind. God's faithfulness to the people already gathered there endures. Faithful innovation is not a repudiation of what has come before, an abandonment of tradition, or a signal that God has forsaken the people already there. It is rather an opportunity to tap the deep roots of God's presence and promises, to renew the identity of the existing church, and to find ways to share those promises with those outside the church—to open up and expand the reach of the gospel.

While Paul and his companions typically began in the local synagogue, sometimes they met with resistance and were thrown out. This pushed them to form relationships with gentiles. Paul may have done this in his vocation as a tentmaker, setting up or joining a local guild where he could listen and share with others as they worked. You may discover that some members of your congregation aren't interested in the faithful innovation journey—at least not initially. You might get more people on board later. This is fine. It's best to start small with a group of people from the congregation who are willing to try new things. Don't expect everyone to join at the same pace.

It is also vital to note that the journey we're describing takes time to transform the culture of the congregation. While the Listen-Act-Share practices can be introduced and piloted as a cycle over nine months to a year, their widespread adoption in an existing congregation can take much longer. Changing the culture of any kind of organization typically takes years, and changing congregational culture can take even longer. So it is crucial to take the long view and be patient on this journey.

## Following Curiosity and Wonder

When we listen to God, to Scripture, to our stories in community, and to our neighbors, and when we begin to wonder what God might be up to in our neighborhoods, we move from a rigid posture of "fixing" to a more helpful posture of curiosity. We spend less time trying to manage our way through technical solutions[1] to a prede-termined destination and more time getting caught up in a journey of spiritual discovery and encounter, like the one we see in Acts 16. Such a shift involves *unlearning* because many congregations are far more used to coming up with plans to manage their way into a new future than engaging in an improvisational journey of spiritual dis-cernment that leads to an unknown destination.

If your congregation defaults toward strategic planning, which is easy to conduct without any reference to God, this may be a stretch. It's important to recognize how strange it may feel to people to ask "God questions" rather than "church questions" and to listen and experiment rather than come up with detailed plans and programs ahead of time. This will feel threatening or disconcerting to some who want the security of knowing where the journey is headed

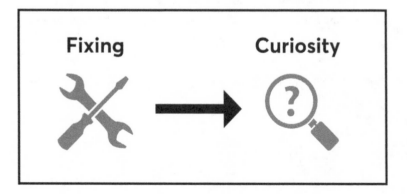

Fixing            Curiosity

before it begins. These are understandable sentiments. As a leader in this process, it can be good to name and acknowledge that this approach can seem strange.

The faithful innovation journey involves a spiritual posture of wonder, openness, and discernment that begins to shift how we go about daily life as disciples as well as how we go about life as a church. Learning to ask "God questions" rather than just "church questions" brings a dimension of necessary humility; we must pay careful attention to God, and it is possible that we might get it wrong. We're susceptible to confusing our agendas with God's agenda and therefore must submit ourselves to the disciplines of praying, reading Scripture, and reflecting in community. Some of these may be new collective practices for your congregation, or at least they might be practices that take new forms from what your people are used to.

Asking "wondering" questions is an essential part of this shift. While congregation members often expect leaders to have the answers ahead of time, in the faithful innovation journey, leaders genuinely don't know what will happen. Their job is to help the people do the discovery work, not to solve it for them. Essential questions are those that help people wonder about what God might be up to, notice God's activity, identify life-giving connections with God and neighbors, and cultivate spiritual curiosity. Leadership in this process is more about asking good questions than having all the answers.

## Starting on the Edges

The creative breakthroughs that took place in the early church tended to start on the edges. It was in Antioch that the disciples discovered and embraced the full inclusion of gentiles in the church; the Jerusalem church was slow to learn this and had to be convinced at the Jerusalem Council (Acts 15). Change and innovation worked from the outside in. As you consider faithful innovation in your church, prepare to begin on the margins rather than the center and expect to be changed from the outside in.

In reality, this typically looks like a small team of people who try out the practices of Listen-Act-Share with others in the congregation. In most cases, that team does not include members of the church board (who must focus on governing the church) or the pastoral staff (who must tend to existing operations). These teams should be led by everyday disciples (lay people), not clergy. It is best to focus experiments on peripheral elements in your church. Don't focus on the primary worship service, for example, where the stakes for change and "failure" are really high. Initiate the work in a space with few existing tasks and moderate-to-low expectations. Invite some people to join you who are relatively open to taking the risk of doing something new.

Over time, as the practices of faithful innovation take hold and people experience them across the life of the congregation, the energy will begin to shift. Rather than looking to leaders to bring the energy to catalyze participation in church activities and programs, people will discover a sense of empowerment in engaging in grassroots practices of listening to Scripture, sharing stories, making greater connections with neighbors, and reflecting together on what they're learning. The energy of the Spirit of God will begin to animate the community in new ways.

This will lead to a transformation of congregational culture. Culture changes when practices (new behaviors) become habits. If a congregation's default method to address a challenge is creating a plan and launching a program, people will shift instead to listening to God and neighbors first and then trying small experiments and reflecting on them. An example would be the goal of reaching young families in the neighborhood. Many churches have launched family-oriented services, hired youth and family ministry staff, and invested significant resources in programming without ever listening first to the young families in their neighborhood to see what they're actually yearning for or without ever seeking God's guidance on what steps to take. It's no surprise that such efforts often fail! Learning and discerning through listening and small experiments may lead in a very different direction. We must be open to the unexpected and ready to be changed by our listening and learning.

The faithful innovation journey also begins to call into question how congregations currently spend their time and energy. One exercise we do with churches is called a Participation Analysis, which invites ministry leaders to consider how their church programs or activities contribute to faith formation. Many of the congregations that have done this exercise have discovered that much of what they spend significant time on doesn't actually yield deeper connections with God, one another, or their neighbors.

---

The Participation Analysis exercise considers a current church program or activity and asks, *What must people know in order to participate? How would participating for six or twelve months impact someone's faith formation and spiritual growth? How would you know if someone was growing spiritually as a result of participating?*

---

We have found that congregations on the faithful innovation journey often experience a refocusing and simplification of their congregational life. Rather than seeing this work as yet another thing to add to an already busy calendar, they discover new energy that frees them to abandon programs, activities, and committees that aren't yielding much spiritual fruit. It becomes far easier for people to release old patterns, models, and traditions when they have discovered a more life-giving alternative. This is why it is vital to start small and "on the side" with faithful innovation practices. As momentum and energy build, it will be much easier to discern what else in congregational life might be pruned or set aside, even temporarily.

## Learning to Ride the Backwards Bicycle

Even though faithful innovation can bring dynamism and joy to a congregation, we want to acknowledge again that congregational change can be difficult for many people. Here is an illustration that we've used to demonstrate just how challenging this can be.

Destin Sandlin, an aerospace engineer and host of the instructional science website Smarter Every Day, set out to learn how to ride a bicycle made by some of his welder friends.[2] What's different about this bicycle is that when you turn the handlebars, the wheel moves in the opposite direction from normal (i.e., if you turn the handlebars to the left, the front wheel moves to the right). Sandlin saw this as a challenge that he could easily overcome. But it took him *eight months* of practice in his driveway—including a fair amount of spills—before he mastered it. His young son was able to learn to ride the backwards bicycle within two weeks—a reflection of how much more flexible young minds are. Sandlin has taken the backwards bicycle around the world and invited all kinds of people to try riding it, and nobody can do it without extensive practice.

We sometimes show the video of the backwards bicycle to church leaders because it illustrates how hard the shift we're describing can feel for people. If you're used to doing church in one mode your whole life, the practices of faithful innovation can feel very strange, like riding a backwards bicycle. It can take time for people to learn how to Listen, Act, and Share, and struggle and failure are

normal parts of the process. In some ways, what's needed is a rewir-
ing of our brains and habits—a deep unlearning as well as a learning
of new things. This is why the discipline of sticking to the practices
repeatedly is so essential. Like learning a language or musical instru-
ment, practice provides the space and structure for transformation
over time. This is God's work; as practices place us repeatedly in
God's presence, God enacts the changes and reveals the next steps
on the journey.

Once congregations get used to the practices of faithful innovation, they can utilize them for whatever challenge or opportunity
they're facing. We witnessed transformative change in a Lutheran
women's organization in Wisconsin. The group was composed entirely
of older members who were frustrated that none of the younger
women were interested in joining. They hadn't considered how their
meeting time—in the middle of a workday—might impact their desired
audience. But they were also struggling with the fact that many of
their own children and grandchildren weren't active in church.

So their faithful innovation coach helped them reframe their
"church question" of *how do we get more women to join our organization?* to a "God question" of *what might God be up to in the spiritual
lives of our children and grandchildren, and how can we join in?* They
started by listening to their own daughters, asking them where
they experienced God in daily life. They discovered that mealtimes
and bedtime were particularly important moments of spiritual connection and reflection in young families. Having heard this, the
older women did some small experiments. They created simple conversation cards for families to use at mealtimes with a short Bible
story, reflection question, and prayer. Then they sewed pockets on
some teddy bears and put personalized prayers in the pockets for
their grandchildren and other children to pull out at bedtime. These
became known as "prayer bears." Through the process, their initial

frustration was redirected toward deeper spiritual connections that pointed to where God was already at work in their children's and grandchildren's lives.

Congregations that take these steps may find themselves going outside the city gates—as Paul did in Acts 16—or outside the walls of the church and spending more time and energy beyond the building. It becomes less important to get people to join church programs and activities and more important to come alongside what God is already doing in the lives of neighbors. The cycles of listening, experimenting, and reflecting become habitual as we take further steps in discernment and discovery. Each cycle leads to the next. Along the way, we find that church is changing in life-giving ways.

## Beginning Outside the Gates

There was no synagogue in Philippi. When Paul and his companions arrived there, they couldn't begin within the established religious structures. Instead, they had to find a place where people were already meeting to pray and seek God. They spent several days in the city before they tried going outside the gates to the river, where women were gathering on the Sabbath for spiritual connection and support. This was a different starting point than some of the other cities they visited on their journeys, where they had launched their work in the synagogue.

You may find yourself starting outside the gates as well—outside the inherited structures of congregational and denominational life. In a time when fewer and fewer Lydias (our spiritually curious neighbors) are looking to enter or join established religious organizations, followers of Jesus must do what Paul and his companions did: discover the "place of prayer" (Acts 16:13) in their own neighborhoods and show up where people are gathering to seek spiritual meaning and connection. Rather than trying to get people to spend more of their lives within the programs and activities of church, church must go to where life is already being lived. We are being called to step out into the community and be present so we can listen, form relationships with neighbors, and hear their stories, struggles, and dreams.

> " Rather than trying to get people to spend more of their lives within the programs and activities of church, church must go to where life is already being lived. "

This involves the practice of being hosted. When we go into the neighborhood with "no purse, no bag, no sandals," as the disciples were called by Jesus to do in Luke 10:4, we go in vulnerability. We must depend on the hospitality of neighbors for our well-being, as Paul and his companions did with Lydia. It was Lydia who hosted them in her home. This shifts the power dynamics considerably. As long as churches stay behind the walls and doors of their buildings, they will remain disconnected from many of their spiritually curious and hungry neighbors. Faithful innovation involves investing presence and relationship in the neighborhood spaces where life plays out.

## Embracing the Mixed Ecology

In Western European nations with long legacies of state churches, such as the United Kingdom, the inherited system of local, geographically based congregations no longer meaningfully connects with the vast majority of neighbors. While most of those neighbors don't mind that a historic church building is part of the cultural landscape, they have no interest in participating in what goes on there. Over the past few decades, churches in those contexts have developed a vision for a "mixed" or "blended ecology" of inherited and new forms of Christian community coexisting together. What began originally in the Church of England as "fresh expressions" of church have now spread worldwide.[3]

Rather than assume a one-size-fits-all approach to what Christian community should look like, the Fresh Expressions movement emphasizes a variety of different forms that meet people where they are. For instance, there are Christian communities started among families with young children ("Messy Church"), for people who share hobbies or interests (biker church, runner church), within public spaces (café church, dinner church, forest church), or as part of a social network (such as families affiliated with a school). These expressions are all relatively simple in their practices and far more culturally accessible than traditional churches.

Fresh expressions of church begin wherever people are already living life. Christians invest presence and relationship there, initially by listening; then by loving, serving, and building community; and eventually by exploring discipleship with those who are interested in doing so. Rather than trying to get these neighbors back into the structures of the inherited church, new forms of Christian community take shape within neighborhood spaces. This means different things in different contexts and results in a multitude of Christian communities of various sizes and shapes that fit into the diversity of how people live life today. Within a mixed ecology, traditional inherited churches have their place, but not as the only option for reaching people.

Fresh expressions are connected to the larger church system under structures of accountability, but more in a network structure than in a traditional hierarchy. Fresh expressions are not expected

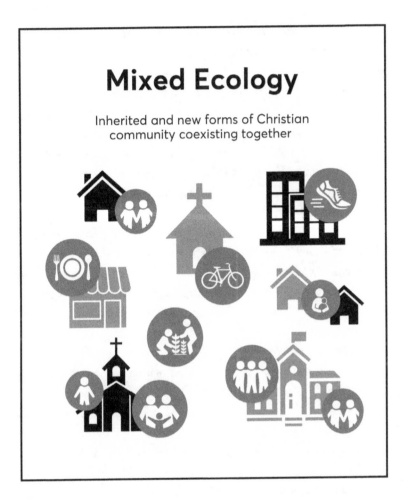

# Mixed Ecology

Inherited and new forms of Christian
community coexisting together

to fit into the old boxes of what church should look like. They carry
forward simple, essential Christian practices, such as Bible study,
prayer, fellowship, and service. Yet they thrive where traditional
churches have little credibility or access. Some are birthed out of
inherited congregations and might arise on the margins of established church life or within the same geographical space. Others

begin from scratch as small groups of pioneer leaders initiate expressions of church within their existing social networks or intentionally inhabit community gathering spaces.

In a mixed ecology, there is a symbiotic relationship between inherited forms and new forms of Christian community. Inherited congregations can initiate and support fresh expressions, and fresh expressions can help bring new learning and vitality to established forms of church. Through all this, we must keep in mind that the church is an organic, living entity. Cycles of death and rebirth are normal parts of the church's life cycle. We should never assume a particular expression of church will endure forever in a particular place, especially given the constant nature of cultural change. It's much easier to embrace a full hospice ward in a hospital when the maternity ward is packed and thriving. As some expressions of church die, new forms will arise to take their place in the larger ecology.

> " Cycles of death and rebirth are a normal part of the church's life cycle. "

In our experience, far too little energy and attention are dedicated to birthing and nurturing new forms of Christian community that are uniquely designed for today's world. Most church leaders at both the local and regional (or national) levels spend the vast majority of their time trying to sustain and revitalize inherited forms of church. This is understandable, as these forms are meaningful and precious, with extensive traditions that can date back hundreds of years. They also tend to bear within them the bulk of the church's existing membership and resources. But while starting new expressions of church is inherently risky, it is actually far riskier to bet on achieving a transformation of the inherited church that was designed for a different era. The odds of success are much lower. Yet that is what we see leaders mostly doing.

As you consider a fresh expression of the church, good questions to ask would include, *If you were designing a form of church to reach spiritually curious but religiously unaffiliated people in your context, what would it look like? Where and when would it meet? What cultural languages would it speak or forms would it take? What questions would it help people answer? What practices would it embrace? How would it stay rooted in the ancient gospel and make that message come alive in ways people could understand?* Your answers to these questions would probably not lead you to come up with what most inherited congregations look like in your area.

The shift from the Age of Association to the Age of Authenticity described in chapter 1 serves as important background to this discussion. If the legacy voluntary association paradigm of the local church is being eroded by cultural forces beyond our control, we need to discover alternatives that can thrive within today's Age of Authenticity. These models of church will likely require less institutional maintenance work on the part of participants. They may be much simpler and more organizationally streamlined, with less of a hierarchical structure, lighter overhead, and fewer costs. They may not even own a building or have staff whose primary livelihood comes from the church. They will center on opportunities to form genuine relationships and explore tough questions together in community. They will do essential things that Christians have always done in various times and places but with perhaps fewer of the social and cultural activities that characterize inherited churches.

There is no "right" way to do this, no one-size-fits-all approach. That is the point of a mixed ecology. Imagine a garden in which multiple and various expressions of Christian community and witness are seeded, planted, and watered and take shape. Some will thrive, and others won't; that is to be expected. The key is to learn along the way. This is where the faithful innovation process is so valuable. Through it, we listen, discern, try small experiments, reflect, and learn.

In Mark 4:1-20, Jesus tells a parable about a sower scattering seed. Some of the seed falls on the path and is eaten by birds. Other seed falls on rocky ground and never takes root. Some seed falls among thorns and is choked by them. However, the seed that falls into good soil yields an exponential abundance of growth. This metaphor helps us keep perspective on the process of cultivating experimental forms of Christian community. We can expect many of our experiments to "fail"; that is normal. There are cultural and social conditions that thwart the flourishing of Christian communities. Yet there is no lack of seed. The sower is incredibly generous and willing to take the risk of spreading the word of God widely. We should embrace a similar imagination.

## Leadership in the Mixed Ecology

If the church needs a mixed ecology of diverse experiments in Christian community that can coexist in today's contexts, we must think more expansively about leadership. Most inherited models of church leadership are too restrictive for the situation we find ourselves in. In many global majority contexts where the church is growing and thriving, pastors are significantly outnumbered by local evangelists and other lay leaders who start and tend churches week to week. One of the key learnings from the Fresh Expressions movement is the centrality of everyday disciples as the primary leaders. In fact, the Church of England has discovered that the most effective leaders who start fresh expressions are typically those without formal theological training or ordination.[4]

This should not surprise us. These leaders are embedded within the relational networks and cultural spaces where life plays out. Ordained leaders are too often consumed by managing the established church and don't have the freedom to invest time and presence in neighborhood spaces. Formal theological training can make it difficult for ordained leaders to speak the language of ordinary people. Seminaries tend to teach the language of church tradition without helping seminarians translate that language into accessible forms that people in the neighborhood can understand. Everyday disciples have more credibility than clergy in many contexts where the church is regarded with suspicion.

For these reasons and more, a faithful future of innovative expressions of church will be primarily lay led and clergy supported. For many regular members of the inherited church, this is a strange concept that goes against the grain of their expectations. Their experience of church has conditioned them to think that their role is primarily to support the institutional church through joining, giving, volunteering on committees, and more. The pastor's role, meanwhile, is to perform the faith *for* them by doing the praying, Bible reading, evangelism, and justice work, to name a few. This inherited paradigm is what we call a *performative* model of ministry—the "ministers" or clergy perform the faith for the people.

> " A faithful future of innovative expressions of church will be primarily lay led and clergy supported. "

What is needed instead is a more participatory *formative* paradigm of ministry where clergy focus on cultivating discipleship and ministry among the whole people of God. Without robust practices of discipleship, everyday believers within the body of Christ will not experience the transformation that life in Christ brings or be able to share that transformation with their neighbors. Our experience has taught us that many inherited congregations function primarily as social and cultural institutions rather than disciple-making communities. Cultivating intentional spiritual growth as followers of Jesus is not what the congregation is focused on or designed around. There is no clear vision of what following Jesus looks like in daily life or access to practices by which people can continue to grow spiritually. It is this model of inherited church that is increasingly running out of steam as the culture moves away from Age of Association institutions. If there is no clear, shared spiritual purpose and vitality, neighbors will not be interested in participating.

Shifting from a performative to a formative model of ministry involves significant unlearning for congregations. It is a renegotiation of the basic social contract that has governed the lives of people in those churches. Many of these members never agreed to pray with others, read the Bible themselves, share their faith stories with

## Models of Ministry

|  | Performative | Formative |
|---|---|---|
| **Leaders** | Primarily perform faith for the people in the congregation | Primarily cultivate discipleship among the whole people of God |
| **People** | Focus on supporting the institutional church | Actively own their spiritual growth |

people in their lives, or start new expressions of Christian community. Their congregation may not have ever addressed these practices or offered guidance on how to do them. In those cases, there will be understandable fear, confusion, and shame.

This significantly shifts the work of pastors and other formally trained leaders toward equipping and empowering the whole people of God in the life of faith. In many congregations, the clergy are the focus of holiness, attention, decision-making, and power. Many people are happy to defer to them. But the journey of faithful innovation requires a different approach. It intentionally provides opportunities for the whole people of God to try on spiritual practices and live more deeply into their identity as followers of Jesus in everyday encounters. The pathway of Christian discipleship moves from the ministry leader to the congregation as a whole.

The simple practices of faithful innovation offer a starting point for that journey for congregation members. Dwelling in the Word, listening to spiritual stories, paying spiritual attention to daily life in the neighborhood, and asking "God questions" all provide accessible avenues for people to deepen their spiritual lives and build their capacity to join what God is doing in their contexts. We have seen congregations transformed as people become more comfortable with these practices and begin to use them apart from formal church activities. For instance, in one congregation, a lay leader who had not previously been very comfortable with interpreting the Bible found Dwelling in the Word so powerful that when her father died and the family gathered, she led them in this practice as a way to identify God's hope amid their loss.

For leaders beginning outside the inherited church, the listening, discernment, and experimenting practices of faithful innovation are ways in which neighbors can be engaged from the start. The very process of planting a church changes too. Rather than trying to begin a new Christian community by predetermining what it should look like and then trying to market or sell that vision to neighbors, leaders can start by listening to those neighbors' spiritual stories, engaging them in interpreting Bible stories imaginatively, and trying out small experiments together in spiritual practices and service. The Spirit of God works through the neighbors to shape what the new expression of church will become.

## Lydia's Leadership

Lydia is the kind of leader who is already outside of the inherited church structure. After Paul baptized her and her household, Paul and his companions went and stayed with them. The end of Acts 16 records how Lydia's house became a center for the believers in Philippi. Paul and Silas had been imprisoned and were then miraculously released. Acts 16:40 reads, "After leaving the prison they went to Lydia's home, and when they had seen and encouraged the brothers and sisters there, they departed." Paul and Silas were comfortable enough with Lydia—and the other new believers who had been baptized—carrying forward this new expression of church in Philippi that they moved on and left the church in Lydia's hands. This was Paul's practice throughout his missionary journeys; he raised up local leaders and resisted allowing these new churches to become overly dependent upon him.

Lydia in this story is someone who experienced the power of the gospel but didn't have much formal theological training, credentialing, or insider status in the inherited church. If you identify with her, then God can work powerfully through you. Your neighborhood connections, relationships, and knowledge may be integral to what God wants to do in your context. The fact that you feel marginal to the inherited church may actually be a profound gift, as you may have more freedom than established leaders to experiment, reenvision, innovate, and cultivate the forms of Christian community that God desires.

We believe it is through the spiritually open and curious people within existing congregations—and within our wider neighborhoods—that the Holy Spirit will create new forms of Christian community that embody a faithful and meaningful witness in today's world. God will still work through inherited church structures and has not abandoned God's people there. But those structures are not sufficient for this moment. We need a far more expansive ecology of multiple forms of church coexisting, where everyday disciples can live more fully into their identity in Christ, deepen their participation in God's life, and share the hope that is within them with their neighbors without expecting church professionals to do it for them. How might such an ecology come to flourish? It will require a very different approach to leadership on the part of those within the inherited church. The next chapter will explore what that looks like.

# Six

## Faithful Innovation as a Way of Leading

It was 11:15 p.m. on a Saturday night, and Pastor Miguel was struggling to wrap up his sermon for the Sunday morning worship service. He kept thinking about what a difficult week it had been for his tiny congregation. One of his oldest and most generous members had passed away, and as Miguel led the funeral service, he wondered how the church would survive without its biggest financial supporter. Those thoughts drifted once more to Miguel's mind as he stared at the half-finished sermon on the screen in front of him. He felt guilty that he was always so worried about money. Sometimes it seemed like there was little time for anything else as the church moved from one crisis to another. On top of everything, the roof over the sanctuary was leaking again, and two of his council members had been bitterly arguing with each other about how to fix it. Miguel was exhausted, and he was beginning to wonder whether he could keep going at this pace. He hadn't imagined being constantly faced with these kinds of problems when he became a pastor. As the night stretched on, he questioned his future. Was this how ministry was supposed to be?

———————————

Lee had just put her kids to bed and cleaned up the kitchen after dinner. She now had a few quiet moments to put the finishing touches on the Sunday school lesson for her class of ten- and eleven-year-olds. Lee loved serving as a leader in her church, but sometimes the demands of her career and family overwhelmed her and made it tough to find time to prepare. This week had been particularly intense at her job. Lee wanted to give her all as a teacher. She felt she was doing God's work and that this was an important calling on her life. But there were definitely times when she felt ill-equipped or just too exhausted to serve. She didn't know where to turn with her concerns. Lee wanted the energy, hope, and abundant life that she knew God had promised. Where could she find it?

———————————

Many of the church leaders we've worked with, no matter their role in the congregation, report feeling depleted and distracted. We've heard story after story about their sense of exhaustion and frustration. At its best, ministry is life-giving. Yet for these leaders, the work they're doing has become anything but. There is a general sense among both ordained and lay leaders that the responsibilities of ministry are overwhelming and insurmountable. They are wondering if what they do actually makes a difference in the lives of the people in their faith communities or neighborhoods.

These concerns are true for congregations that are struggling with issues like dwindling membership and shrinking financial contributions, but they can show up in thriving and growing churches too. The same undercurrent of uncertainty affects both because something is fundamentally broken. This reality leads to questions: *Why are so many people struggling to lead the church? Why are seemingly healthy congregations still wrestling with the same issues as those in decline? How can church leaders of all kinds even consider beginning a journey of faithful innovation when they are one problem or crisis away from abandoning ministry entirely?*

The journey of faithful innovation is intentionally designed to focus on the everyday disciples in congregations. This keeps the learning and growth where it must be located—among the whole people of God. In our experience, ministry leaders don't need one more thing to manage and run or one more task to accomplish on behalf of the congregation. Yet those leading the church have a vitally important role to play in the faithful innovation journey. Much of what happens in today's congregations—decisions about programming, staffing, worship style, and even neighborhood outreach—flows from the people in leadership roles. When those leaders are struggling, faithful innovation can seem like just another obligation to add to the growing pile.

We've seen firsthand how widespread the challenges are for all kinds of leaders in all kinds of churches, and we want to offer hope that things can be different. If you serve as a ministry leader in any capacity, this chapter is for you. We will address what faithful innovation looks like for ordained and lay leaders as well as for church staff. We will also explore how you can embrace practices that contribute not only to your congregation's flourishing as it innovates faithfully but also to your own flourishing as you lead this work.

## Preparing Your People for Faithful Innovation

The journey of faithful innovation within a congregation is about transformative change, which means adopting some new things while leaving some old things behind. Even in the most ideal circumstances, change of any kind can be difficult for the people in your congregation. You might experience pushback from your members, from your church council, or even from other leaders or colleagues. If this happens, it may actually indicate that you're doing something right. Change inherently brings discomfort and uncertainty, and this kind of response might signal that a shift is taking place.

Part of the difficulty of change stems from the loss that accompanies it. Your people might experience the loss of the familiar, or they may even anticipate a loss that has yet to arrive. The members of our faith communities have strong ties to how things are usually done, particularly if those elements have long histories. It's normal for them to resist or struggle when they are faced with the prospect or reality of losing something important to them. They might also be struggling with losses that extend beyond the church. It can seem like all of life is in turmoil these days. Crises that are close to home or events on the national or world stage can create anxiety that cripples our ability to move forward. Your community may not be able to step into God's hopeful future until this heartache is addressed. Your role as a leader is to listen to the longings and losses[1] of those you serve and create spaces where their thoughts and feelings can be explored in light of the gospel. You are uniquely positioned to guide your people toward the unknown but hopeful future God is calling them into.

One of the exercises that we've developed with our colleagues and used with congregational leaders is Listening to Longings and Losses, which is a variation of the ancient practice of lament. It allows people to express their fears and hopes together as a community. You can also practice it yourself to process your own concerns about what God might be calling you to relinquish in your ministry. The expression of our longings and losses follows the pattern of lament found in the Psalms, where the writer addresses a complaint to God in the form of a prayer.[2] You might name to God what you long for and wish were true about your congregation as well as your fears about what might be or has been lost. Then you confess your need for God's grace and forgiveness while asking God for help. Your prayer of lament concludes with an expression of trust that God will lead you and the congregation and a commitment that you will praise God for how God has delivered you. This ancient practice provides a necessary outlet for the pain you and your people might be experiencing while placing God at the center by naming God as the one we can turn to in our suffering.

> The practice of Listening to Longings and Losses processes a congregation's lament by asking, *What is one hope you have for the congregation? What used to happen in the congregation that you wish would return? What do you fear might be lost as the congregation moves into the future?*

## Reconnecting with Your Own Source of Life

Maybe you've been leading at your church for decades, or maybe you are still in your first call or in your first ministry leadership role. Perhaps you are somewhere in between. You might be serving as a leader at a church in decline. Or you might be at a church experiencing rapid growth. No matter how long you've been serving in your present role, and no matter what is happening in your congregation, you are likely searching for a better way to do ministry. You are here, reading this chapter, because you can tell that something is missing or that God is calling you to something more or something new.

Take a moment to think back to why you originally took on your present role. What were the reasons you decided to become a leader in Christian ministry? Did you have a sense of God's calling on your life? Were you eager to share the word of God? Did you want to care for others and walk beside them in their moments of deepest need? Were you excited about helping people see the difference Jesus can make in their everyday lives?

We're guessing you probably didn't opt to become a ministry leader so you could navigate your way through church politics or stretch yourself thin among many competing obligations. Leading a congregation on a journey of faithful innovation means you are helping people discover a new way of being the church. At the same time, it is an opportunity to rediscover your own passion and calling. When was the last time you really thought about your love for God? How long has it been since you spent time tending to your own relationship with Jesus?

Some of the core work for ministry leaders is getting back in touch with who God is and how your own story—and the congregation's story—connects with the larger narrative of God's redemptive work in the world. It means letting God's purposes speak into and direct how you live your life as well as impact the choices you make about your ministry. It also means prioritizing your own spiritual journey. Your spiritual health as a leader is the crucial foundation for a vibrant, thriving congregation.

It's all too easy for us to conflate accomplishing things for God with spending quality time with God. For some of us, this is the root of where our troubles begin as leaders. We are charged with helping others grow in their faith—with developing Christian disciples.

But as pastor Peter Scazzero notes, "We cannot give what we do not possess."[3] He wisely insists that "work *for* God that is not nourished by a deep interior life *with* God will eventually be contaminated by other things. . . . The joy of Christ gradually disappears."[4] We are able to draw up and serve the life-giving water of the Holy Spirit to our congregations when our own well is nourished and flourishing.

If you've ever flown anywhere on an airplane, you've heard the instructions from the flight attendants about putting on your own oxygen mask before you attempt to help others. This idea of filling our own tank first, of replenishing our well, is very apt for ministry. We serve the church out of energy that comes from God's Spirit. When we no longer can claim our own experience of the love of Jesus, that's a signal to us that something is broken. Returning our attention to God becomes an urgent matter of survival. Fortunately, we can draw on the long history of the Christian tradition for some practical solutions to this problem.

## Using Spiritual Practices to Reconnect with God

Spiritual practices date back to the early church, and many have their origins in Jewish rituals that were observed by the ancient nation of Israel. In previous chapters, we shared a wide variety of practices that are designed to engage both you and the congregation together as a community. In this chapter, we've turned our attention to practices that are intended to nourish you as a leader. We already included one of these (Listening to Longings and Losses) in the preceding section.

Why are spiritual practices so essential for Christian leaders? These timeless disciplines are the vehicles through which God renews, empowers, and changes us, preparing us to effectively tackle all kinds of ministry challenges. It is not the practices themselves that are important but what they do for us that matters. Spiritual practices place us in God's presence so God can do transforming work within us through the power of the Spirit. The emphasis is on God's agency rather than our own.

> " Spiritual practices place us in God's presence so God can do transforming work within us through the power of the Spirit. "

Yet our personal agency does come into play through the choices we make. We decide, for example, how we want to spend our time and what actions we want to take. Growth is inevitable for humans—we continue to change and develop throughout our lives. The question is whether we are growing in a direction that will ultimately lead us into deeper Christ-likeness. In our relationships with other people, we often become incrementally more like those who are close to us, subtly taking on their characteristics and mannerisms. People might even remark that they can tell we've been spending time with so-and-so. The same is true in our relationship with Christ. As we come near to God and repeatedly find ourselves located in God's presence through our spiritual practices, we begin to speak and act in ways that are more Christ-like. We start to affirm what God affirms and love the people God loves. These changes can become noticeable to others as our lives become out of step with our surrounding culture. If people begin to notice something odd about the way you live and love, that might be evidence that God is doing something powerful inside of you.

Becoming like Christ is the goal of every Christian. This is why the faithful innovation journey repeatedly emphasizes spiritual practices. As we've led ordained and lay leaders through this process, we've seen firsthand how transformative the practices can be in the spiritual lives of leaders. One pastor we worked with told us about the moment when he discovered he was not very good at noticing God's presence in his everyday life. He admitted he was initially fearful; he wondered how he could help his people do something that he himself was unable to do. This realization prompted him to adopt new spiritual practices that have deepened his own walk with Jesus. He came away from the process with a profound understanding of how attending to his own spiritual health helped him be a better pastor for his congregation. For him, his spiritual development was no longer optional but had become a core part of his ministry. He realized he needed his own foundation in God before he could help his congregation establish theirs.

How do you experience God? Exploring this question is the first step to finding—or rediscovering—your own spiritual rhythm. In order to grow spiritually, you must discover not only who God is but also who *you* are. Your temperament, likes and dislikes, skills and passions, and experiences and goals all contribute to determining which of the spiritual practices can help you become more attuned to God's presence. There is a rich menu of practices to choose from, like Dwelling in the Word or other ancient spiritual disciplines like silence and solitude or fasting. Different practices resonate with different people, and part of the journey is discovering which ones best help you connect with God. If something works for you, keep doing it. If it draws you further away from God, lay it down. You might return to it at a later point, and it might prove useful then.

We've encouraged leaders to use the spiritual practice of Examen[5] to discern where God has been at work in their lives. This practice invites us to consider the various places where we've recently noticed God's activity. We become aware of God's presence in the moment, and then we reflect on the life-giving and the life-taking moments in our recent days and weeks, which respectively draw us closer or further away from God. As you consider where you're seeing God, you'll get better at recognizing God's activity not only in your own life but also in the lives of the people in your congregation. This practice strengthens your discernment so you can better lead others.

> The practice of Examen asks, *How are you experiencing God's presence in this moment? What was the most life-giving in the previous day or week that brought you closer to God and others? What was the most life-taking that drew you apart from God and others?*

## Building Your Support Network

It can be lonely in ministry. Do you have people you can turn to for help with leadership challenges or your own mental or emotional well-being? Often, these will be other leaders or clergy outside your church community, or they might be spiritual directors, coaches, counselors, or other professionals. It can be difficult, and sometimes inadvisable, to share your concerns with the people in your congregation. External listening partners might be in the best position to identify with your challenges and offer advice, solutions, or just a friendly listening ear. Sometimes these supportive colleagues may arise in unexpected places. It is possible and healthy for leaders to forge tight bonds across denominations, demographics, theological leanings, political affiliations, and other boundaries that usually serve to separate us from one another. When we seek listening partners who are not like us, we experience the richness of God's community. We also flex our curiosity as we learn how to practice conversations across differences. This is a skill our church desperately needs in these divisive times.

It can be particularly helpful to have a coach who walks alongside you and your congregation throughout the faithful innovation journey. A coach is a listening partner who is trained to ask questions that focus people's attention on God's presence and their own engagement in the process. The coach creates space for difficult conversations, provides opportunities for healing and new growth, and helps people honestly reflect on what they've learned. We recommend that coaches come from outside the congregation so they can offer an independent, unbiased perspective.

Coaches also play a substantial role in learning communities, which provide a communal version of the coaching relationship with multiple listening partners. These peer-to-peer cohorts meet regularly in small groups with a guide to build deep connections, define primary challenges, learn by doing, and engage in reflection. They are safe and encouraging environments where participants can share their most pressing concerns and issues with other leaders in similar roles and contexts. If you would like to learn more about coaching and learning community opportunities from Luther Seminary's Faith+Lead, we've included information in the Resources for the Journey section at the end of the book.

Finding a supportive community is crucial for your role as a leader, and we discovered this for ourselves through an experiment our team started in late 2019, not long before the pandemic began. We convened a weekly Dwelling in the Word webcast for ministry leaders of all kinds, and the original goal was to provide a forum where ordained and lay preachers could share ideas for sermon preparation with one another by dwelling on the lectionary text for the upcoming Sunday. Little did we know how God would use our efforts.

What began as a small gathering soon became a lifeline for around forty people every week as Covid-19 disrupted face-to-face connections. Several of the participants reported how much they came to rely on regularly seeing their fellow ministry leaders every Tuesday. Some began connecting with one another outside of the scheduled weekly time, sharing books and resources through the mail and praying for one another as times of crisis arrived in their lives. One clergy member said the people on Zoom had become like family to her. Week after week, this group of virtual strangers had developed into a community of faith. Although its members were dispersed across the globe and across denominations, they were now an essential support system for one another.

## Reframing Expectations for Yourself and Others

If you are going to refocus your church's energy on faithful innovation, you will immediately face a dilemma. Faithful innovation requires change—taking risks, trying things, exploring the unknown, and staying focused on God's mission. Yet most people in organizations, including the church, want things to stay stable and want leaders to protect them from change. To lead faithful innovation, you must be open to "disappointing people at a rate they can absorb."[6]

 **Reframing Expectations**

| What the congregation expects of leaders | What leaders expect of the congregation |

This is OK. You can't be everything for everyone at every moment. You will wear yourself out if you try.

Think about what you do as a pastor, lay leader, or church staff member during an average week. You might spend time preparing a sermon, which could include meditating on your text, consulting a range of exegetical commentaries, and preaching your message in a way that illuminates God's word for people. Or maybe you're setting up ways for people to explore the neighborhood around your building, helping them learn how to listen to those outside the church to find out what keeps them up at night. Or perhaps you are encouraging the church to reflect on where they are seeing God at work in their lives, and then you're inviting them to share those stories with one another as a way of honoring God in the midst of your community.

These are all examples of vital ministry work that brings the church one step closer to God's hopeful future. But you might read this list with a twinge of envy or guilt. You might be too overwhelmed with other responsibilities to even start thinking about the core of your calling. We've seen this reality countless times in the lives and ministries of the leaders we've walked beside. One pastor compared the weight of her responsibilities to feeling like she was carrying a lopsided layer cake up to the judging table for God to review. She sensed that its collapse might come at any moment, and she worried about needing to fix everything on her own. Through her experiences as part of the faithful innovation journey, she began to realize that the cake—a symbol of her congregation—was not solely hers; Jesus was carrying it beside her, and she was not actually responsible for its success or failure. She also wasn't alone; the entire church was meant to be part of this work. Even if something *did* fail, God would be there to help.

This pastor needed liberation from the tyranny of expectations— from her congregation and even from herself—before she could take the journey of faithful innovation. Other leaders are tied down by quotas and metrics and budgets and buildings. They are so focused on running the inherited church that they've lost their missional imagination. They can't see what God is up to. Maybe you've been there before, or maybe you're there right now. Please hear us: other leaders have been where you are. They found hope as they embarked on the faithful innovation journey, shedding the unnecessary and drawing closer to God. This is reminiscent of the way God removes unfruitful branches from the vine so it can flourish (John 15:2).

So how might you trim what isn't needed from your ministry? In your role as a leader, you might be taking care of things for your people that they could or should be doing for themselves. The early church embodied the concept of the priesthood of all believers (1 Pet 2:9) by functioning as a unified whole where every member played their part in the body of Christ. This was a participatory or formative model of church that engaged everyone in the work of discipleship. However, many churches over the centuries have come to adopt a *performative* model where professional clergy act out the important elements of faith to a watching congregation. Many people come to church on Sundays for an experience that is largely transitory and goes no further than the immediate moment. They are dependent upon their pastors to essentially do their spiritual growing for them. This puts an intense burden on ministry leaders.

Faithful innovation envisions a church where everyone—not just pastors or lay leaders—is actively involved in God's work and mission. How you define your own leadership role is paramount for how you will function within your church. If you see yourself as "at the center"—as the beginning and end of your ministry—you will try to do everything yourself. This is the pathway that leads to burnout. It is not the fruitful life that God desires for you.

> " Faithful innovation envisions a church where everyone—not just pastors or lay leaders—is actively involved in God's work and mission. "

You are a finite human with limitations. You cannot do everything everyone asks of you, and the best part of this is that you actually don't have to.[7] God invites us to prioritize our ministry work according to his mission. We can look to Jesus as our example. He did not accomplish every task set before him. Crowds gathered around him wherever he went, and many were looking for miraculous healings. Yet Jesus often left while the crowd was still gathered (Matt 8:18; 13:36). Jesus selectively healed certain individuals while leaving others unhealed (John 5:1–15). As Messiah, he didn't overthrow the Roman government like people thought he would. Many of the Jews were shocked when he died instead, and it wasn't even a noble death. Jesus died shamefully on a cross. He disappointed scores of people who left his presence with their expectations of him unfulfilled.[8]

One of the exercises we do with ministry leaders is an Expectations Analysis where we ask them to list all the expectations that people have for them and their own expectations of themselves in their role. This is typically a very long list—far more than anyone could ever fulfill. Then we ask them to list what the church expects of its regular members. This is always a much shorter list that usually focuses on supporting the inherited church more than practicing the faith in daily life or being a witness to Jesus in the world. Then we ask clergy and congregation members to reimagine what they *should* be focusing on to help people live as faithful disciples in the world. For leaders in the church, this means reframing and redefining expectations, giving ministry away, and inviting the congregation into a deeper journey of exploration and growth. As you fill your plate with only what is necessary for your role as your congregation's spiritual leader, you will leave some things undone. This means you will need others to help you with the tasks you lay aside.

> The Expectations Analysis exercise helps you reframe inappropriate expectations your congregation might have for you or that you might have for yourself by asking, *What are you doing for your congregation that they could do for themselves? How might you encourage them to take ownership of their own spiritual development?*

## How Sabbath Can Help Us

What did Jesus do when he walked away from his endless to-do list? He spent time in restorative silence and solitude with God, withdrawing to lonely places to pray (Luke 5:16). He took a Sabbath rest. Jesus paused all that he was doing, all that he was responsible for, and surrendered himself to God. Jesus stayed focused on his mission by following God's instructions and entrusting the needs of the people into God's capable hands. He was able to complete the tasks of his public life because he attended to the work of maintaining his inner life. Jesus models the healthiest directional flow of ministry—from God's power, through the Holy Spirit, into our lives as leaders, and then out into the people of congregations, communities, and neighborhoods.

We can follow Jesus's example. For us, taking a break to focus on our spiritual development requires a deep trust that God will take care of everything—and everyone—while we immerse ourselves in God's transforming and healing presence. Sometimes the hardest part of taking a Sabbath break is the first step, where we intentionally set aside all that we need to do in order to seek God. We are asked to trust that God will take care of the needs that we don't meet. We let God take the reins. Not everything that arrives in our inbox or at our doorway is ours to handle. The Holy Spirit can help us discern which tasks are truly ours.

As Ruth Haley Barton reminds us, we lay aside our work for a Sabbath "whether everything has been finished or not."[9] We cannot wait until the point where we feel ready to begin our Sabbath because that time may never come. There is always more to do—the work of ministry can be all-consuming if we let it. The Sabbath rest itself is what sets us free from the expectations of others, from our to-do lists, and from our growing exhaustion. We are invited to join God for a time of renewal and refreshment as we rest. Only then can we again take up the work God has given us to do.

> " The Sabbath rest itself is what sets us free from the expectations of others, from our to-do lists, and from our growing exhaustion. "

> Sabbath is an invitation from God to temporarily lay aside our responsibilities and rest in God's presence. We pause from our work to spend time enjoying God and God's gifts to us.

Moreover, Sabbath is not just for our own benefit. Its dimensions are both personal and communal. We are invited into multiple kinds of surrender as we rest our emotions, our minds, and our physical bodies.[10] But we also affirm the inherent value and dignity of other people as we recognize that they are worth far more than their accomplishments and as we extend the grace and gift of Sabbath rest to those beyond our immediate families, households, and communities.[11] When we create space for others to have opportunities to rest, we fulfill God's command to love our neighbors as ourselves.

## Empowering Everyday Disciples

You already know that you are a leader—if not *the* leader—in your church. But who else is a leader in your congregation? We've seen that you can't do everything yourself. You only have so much time and energy. Faithful innovation asks you to turn your attention back to the core work of cultivating deeper spiritual connections and growth rather than being consumed by trying to manage the institutional ministry of the inherited church. Your focus must shift, so how will you still manage to get everything done?

The answer is that you won't—at least by yourself. You will need to rethink how you define leadership in your church. You have a wealth of untapped potential sitting in your pews every Sunday. The everyday disciples you minister to are the key to helping you take the next step in the faithful innovation journey. When you empower them to take on day-to-day ministry tasks, and even bigger decisions and responsibilities, you are free to embrace your role as the church's spiritual leader.

Faithful innovation asks us to expand our understanding of ministry leadership to include potential leaders who don't fit the mold. They may have limited theological training, or they may have out-of-the-box ideas about ministry. They may want to convene the church in unusual places or establish fresh expressions of church to reach those who wouldn't normally attend a worship service. These everyday disciples are the next generation of ministry leaders, and many of them are primed and waiting for an opportunity to serve. The church needs them just as much as it needs professionally trained pastors. You need these leaders to help you. You might even be one of them yourself. The efforts of ordained and lay leaders combined with everyday disciples—you and the people in your pews—can make faithful innovation possible in almost any context.

If you want to empower the people in your congregation, you might start by helping them discover their own spiritual gifts and talents. Encourage them to take a spiritual gift inventory to help them identify their gifts and how to use them in ministry service. One example is the APEST Personal Vocational Assessment,[12] which draws on Ephesians 4:7, 11–12 to reveal areas of motivation and expression from five different ministry types: apostle, prophet, evangelist, shepherd, and teacher. Once people have taken an inventory, they will need an environment where they can explore possible areas of ministry by matching their talents with the needs of the church as well as with the needs of the community. Those with organizational skills can lead committees. People who are gifted with fostering relationships can be trained to provide pastoral care. Others can take their abilities into their workplaces and homes, living out their callings in a variety of contexts. Give people the freedom to experiment and to gently fail—if things don't go well, the fallout will be minor. When something they try doesn't fit, they can move on to something else. Creating this kind of environment takes patience on your part and trust on the part of your people. It doesn't happen overnight, but the payoff is worth it when you enable an entire team of leaders to join you in ministry.

## Getting Started as a Faithfully Innovative Leader

What does faithfully innovative leadership look like in practice? How do you take the first step? The best place to start is by getting your attention back on God. Ministry work can be overwhelming when we push ahead in our own strength. God's Spirit is there to help us. The pressure of doing the complicated work of ministry without the leading of the Spirit is a sure recipe for burnout. We were never intended to lead God's church on our own without the sustaining power of God.

If we have just our own energy to guide us, we'll quickly get bogged down in the mundane tasks of running and sustaining a church structure. If this sounds soul draining to you, you're in good company! The mission of the church is to make Christian disciples and to reach the world with the gospel message of Jesus Christ. Yet many congregations have lost clarity on their spiritual purpose—their call to participate in God's creative, healing, restoring work in their context—and instead are consumed with managing and sustaining a religious institution. No wonder leaders feel ground down. When God's Spirit is welcomed into our midst, the real work of discipleship moves within reach. What may have seemed humanly impossible before becomes divinely possible as God opens the doors. God travels the road beside us too. As we engage with God through spiritual practices, we invite the power of God's Spirit to indwell us. God accompanies us on this journey.

As you seek God's leading in your life, you'll want to revisit your own call to ministry. Are you serving in a place where you can faithfully grow and serve? Will your community be receptive to the journey of faithful innovation? You will probably encounter roadblocks and frustration as you introduce changes to the congregation. Make sure you have supportive people around you to provide encouragement and to refocus your attention on God's direction. These will often be people outside your congregation and, as we mentioned earlier, could include spiritual directors, coaches, and colleagues in similar leadership roles.

We're in conversation with increasing numbers of leaders who are passionate about cultivating innovative, new forms of Christian community that will meet people where they are in today's world but who find themselves thwarted by bureaucratic, denominational structures and resistance from the inherited church. You may feel that way. Some of these leaders do need to take the courageous step of walking away from these structures to follow God's call in their ministries. We created an incubator/accelerator fellowship program called the Seeds Project to provide support, coaching, and connection for these leaders, as we know it can be a lonely and vulnerable journey. If this describes you, discern carefully what your next step might be. You can find more information about this program in the Resources for the Journey section at the end of the book.

Wherever you are, we invite you to be bold in your efforts to try something new. Convene a team within your church to join you in discerning the movement of the Holy Spirit both inside the church and outside in the broader community. Stay curious and open to where the Spirit directs you. As you consider what to try, keep your experiments affordable and accessible. Listen to the people in your congregation and expect to hear from God in unexpected places and through unexpected people.

None of these things are easy. You might find it hard to get people to the point where they are willing to let some of their cherished traditions go. Maybe you're there right now—you've embraced faithful innovation yourself, but your congregation is unwilling or unable to join you on the journey. This is the point where you are faced with tough decisions. Do you follow the Spirit's leading *wherever* that takes you, or do you tough it out in a role that isn't moving forward? Some of the leaders we've worked with made the difficult choice to change churches, and some even left ministry altogether. You can serve God anywhere—you don't have to be inside the institutional church to do that. But we want to encourage you to exercise careful communal discernment as you consider your passion for your call and patiently discover what God wants for you and your church. The church needs faithfully innovative leaders, and God can help you break through the intractability that may be holding your congregation back.

It's actually not up to us to fix the church or to solve all of the world's problems. We can't make ourselves right either. These things are God's work, and we can trust that God will get it done. Meanwhile, we get the privilege of partnering with God to help people make meaning out of their lives, discover the difference Jesus makes, and find their purpose as members of God's holy and eternal community. This is the hopeful future that faithful innovation points to. We will look at the pathway to reaching that hope in our final chapter.

How to get started with faithful innovation:

- seek God's leading
- discern your call
- find partners
- start something new
- look beyond your church

# Conclusion

## Discovering God's Hopeful Future

A group of regional church judicatory leaders and staff gathered to reflect together on the realities facing the congregations in their systems. Several of the people described significant numbers of congregations in advanced stages of decline with smaller numbers of churches that were stable or thriving. They talked about the struggle to identify, recruit, train, and support healthy leaders. They named the major cultural shifts that were happening all around their churches. One leader spoke up: "Most of our congregations can't identify their source of hope." A silence fell over the room as the others absorbed the weight of this statement. They recognized that it could apply to their systems as well.

---

The congregation had experienced decades of growth by focusing on making fully devoted followers of Jesus. After the longtime pastor retired, the congregation began to realize how much they depended on that pastor's vision and leadership for their direction. They wondered if they would find another pastor who could fill this void. A lot of people in the congregation also wondered if some changes needed to be made. It didn't seem like hoping that a new pastor could bring vision and direction was necessarily the best way into the future. Did they have to be quite so dependent upon a senior leader? Could the congregation be equipped to listen for God's direction together and discover a collective vision? Might there be a different way to engage the next generation than simply finding the next great pastoral leader? Many people thought there might be a better way.

Within a larger regional church system challenged by decline, a cluster of congregations had been engaged in months of listening, prayer, and experimenting in their neighborhoods. Members of these churches had become much more comfortable paying attention to and naming God's presence and movement in their daily experience. They had discovered life-giving connections with neighbors, including families at a nearby school, newly arrived immigrants, and seniors struggling with loneliness. Every few months, teams from across the congregations would gather to share stories, pray, and encourage one another. Out of this journey emerged experiments like street-corner prayer stations, outdoor prayer services in a local park, a mobile food shelf, and dinner church gatherings in a senior center. The closer the congregations drew to God and neighbors, the less concerned they were about their old ways of doing church and the more hopeful they became.

In the earlier chapters of this book, we painted a picture of the inherited church in crisis. Widespread pastoral exhaustion and disengagement from congregational affiliation and participation are signs of deeper cultural shifts underway that can't easily be fixed. Many churches aren't offering a clear identity and story to a society increasingly skeptical of religious institutions. Some churches have adopted identities shaped more by political and cultural tribalism than by the gospel. This may bring a certain kind of energy and engagement from some people, but it only confirms the worst suspicions unchurched neighbors have about how compromised the church has become. They don't see Jesus in it.

Underneath shrinking budgets, burned-out leaders, and ambivalence about mission lies a deeper theological crisis. Many churches can't identify where their hope comes from. They aren't clear on their core story and struggle to experience and name the power of the living God in their midst. If they can't articulate and embody an alternative vision for human wholeness and flourishing, they won't be able to speak to a society that is struggling to identify its own sources of hope and falling into despair.

Where do we find hope? It doesn't come from the church's institutional power, resources, or abilities. For decades, the church has taken its cues from the surrounding culture on what it should care about and how it should operate. At different points in its history over the past seventy-five years, it has been a gathering place at the center of civic life, a driver for social and political change, and an efficiently managed business enterprise. But to the extent to which the church justifies its existence in the world based on these terms, it will struggle to identify its source of hope and fail to faithfully flourish.

The church's identity must be rediscovered and regrounded in the life and power of the triune God. This is where hope is found, and it is a hope that the church must reclaim for itself and offer to the world. God creates the church as a community to embody and give witness to God's love in Christ for humankind and all of creation through the power of the Spirit. For many congregations, the primary work facing them is to learn how to be led by God rather than their own plans, power, and capacities. They cannot thrive apart from God. Such a journey invites us toward a different imagination—a different way of seeing the world. It isn't all up to us. The modern myths that suggest we can live a good life (for ourselves or our churches) apart from God are being shattered by the realities of human suffering, division, and despair. Salvation isn't in our power to grasp; it is a pure gift. We don't need to write our own stories or invent our true selves; we have an identity in Christ that can be neither earned nor lost, no matter what we do. God's grace is *never* exhausted. This is our source of incalculable hope.

> " *The church's identity must be rediscovered and regrounded in the life and power of the triune God.* "

## Losing Your Life to Find It

The church is the earthly community that bears these truths in its collective story through Scripture and through the shared practices that lead people to experience the power of the crucified and risen Christ. Jesus says, "Those who find their life will lose it, and those who lose their life for my sake will find it" (Matt 10:39). We have come through a long period of time in which churches have sought to find their lives in other stories—the stories of organizational success, of activism, of pastoral celebrity, and of institutional growth, to name just a few. These cultural stories are not bad in and of themselves, but they fail to express the church's deeper identity in God. The church must discover what it means to lose its life for Jesus's sake in order to rediscover it.

If you're taking the faithful innovation journey to save your church, we appreciate where that motivation comes from. But as we've alluded to earlier, we believe that focusing on trying to "fix" your church will not actually fix it. The renewal of your church will come through focusing on God and Lydia, not your church. It is through inhabiting the practices of discerning God's presence and movement and paying careful and loving attention to the spiritual seekers in your neighborhood that you will discover new life. That focus will take you on an adventure that will transform how you imagine and embody Christian community. Like the stories of the resurrected Jesus, your church will look different on the other side.

If you're taking the faithful innovation journey because Jesus has changed your life and you want others to know the power of Jesus's love, we encourage you to lean into that experience. You may have a story about how Jesus met you in your despair and loss, offered for-giveness when you were wracked by guilt and shame, or opened doors that seemed impossibly closed. These experiences—and the stories you tell about them—are the lifeblood of the church. We invite you to refocus the church's life around these stories, opening space to share them collectively with the entire congregation. The hope and joy you found are incredible gifts that are meant to be exchanged with the neighbors in your life who are struggling as you once were.

If you're taking the faithful innovation journey because you have Lydias in your life who are searching for hope, meaning, belong-ing, and purpose and who are having a hard time finding them, we encourage you to draw close to those people to hear their stories. Your compassion for people out in the community will connect you with God's heart for their struggles and suffering. Rather than trying to fit those neighbors into the narrowly defined spaces of your congregation, listen to how God might be inviting you to join with them to cultivate forms of Christian community that meet them on their turf and speak their cultural language.

## Don't Go Alone

Though the Listen-Act-Share practices of faithful innovation are simple, the journey itself isn't easy. Just as Paul and his companions wrestled with how the Holy Spirit was leading them even in the face of disappointments, rejections, and redirections, we can expect ambiguity along the way. This is normal and integral to the process of following God. For this and other reasons, don't take the journey alone. Paul and his fellow travelers had the strength and support of walking together as they listened and experimented. When we forge ahead on our own, we are more likely to get distracted and disheartened, and we might be tempted to abandon the journey altogether.

In practice, this means that teams and leaders within local churches should not only collaborate internally but also seek to learn from other church teams in their area or beyond. Stories of God's leading and learning from experiments can spark imagination and inspiration across churches and church systems. In our work at Luther Seminary's Faith+Lead, that has meant connecting congregations into learning communities either regionally or nationally (online) in ways that they can learn from one another. If you feel ready to take the next steps by joining one of these communities to learn or be equipped, go to the Resources for the Journey section at the end of the book to learn more.

## Discovering Hope

As we have walked with churches on this journey over the years, we have seen a rediscovery of hope. This hope does not lie in our ability to transform our church organizationally to be more effective or successful. It does not lie in leaders' energy, charisma, or brilliance. It comes from experiences of the power of the Holy Spirit at the grassroots among the ordinary people of God. What does this look like? It means people being able to listen compassionately to one another in new ways and to hold one another's stories lovingly. It looks like people finding their way into Scripture imaginatively and creatively, where the biblical story begins to reshape how they experience daily life. It looks like taking the risk of showing up in neighborhood spaces and having encounters with people that begin to lead to new relationships. It means following our neighbors' invitations into deeper community and connection. It looks like congregations sharing life-giving stories that free people from nostalgia, fear, and confusion toward new possibilities.

The Spirit of God creates relationships of love and communities of hope. These communities are constituted not by social or cultural uniformity but rather by unity in Christ. The Spirit brings life-giving energy that connects us together across differences. This is what happened with Paul and his companions and to Lydia and her household. The gift and joy of knowing God's unconditional love in Christ freed Paul and his companions from their fears, anxieties, and cultural inhibitions to take an arduous journey to meet Lydia. The Spirit was already at work in Lydia, leading her to be a person of prayer whose heart was open to the gospel. In their encounter, God broke down social and cultural barriers to form a new community. Lydia discovered a new hope. Paul and his companions received from Lydia and her household the gifts of relationship, hospitality, community, and new learnings about what God was up to in Philippi. Everyone was changed by this encounter.

God is at work in your neighborhood and in the lives of your spiritually curious and struggling neighbors. Your church's hopeful future lies not in internal deliberations but rather in going out where life is lived to listen, discern, and discover as you are led by God. You will likely be redirected along the way to meeting your Lydia. But if you listen patiently and persistently to God and your neighbors together, you will find her. You may lose some things in your church's congregational life along the way, but in the process, you'll discover something far more precious.

# Resources for the Journey

As you move forward into faithful innovation, here are tools to help you and your congregation engage in the steps of Listen-Act-Share. We invite you to explore Luther Seminary's **Faith+Lead**, a digital learning hub for Christian leaders who want to connect with God, tell the story of Jesus, cultivate Christian community, practice justice, and shift ministry models in order to be faithful and effective in the twenty-first century.

Visit **faithlead.org** to learn more about the resources listed below.

The **Faithful Innovation Leader Companion** is a hands-on workbook with how-to steps for many of the spiritual practices included in this book. It also has leadership tools and thoughtful exercises designed to be used in a variety of ministry contexts. Available in English and Spanish.

**Faith+Lead Coaching** provides customized, one-on-one pairings between coaches and clients that are grounded in respectful and careful listening. Highly trained coaches—who understand the unique demands of ministry—offer personalized support in a wide range of categories that include self-care, well-being, goal setting, accountability, relationships, leadership, and more.

**Faith+Lead Learning Communities** combine small-group coaching with facilitated peer cohorts in a multimonth learning journey that includes in-person and online gatherings, guided experiments in the participants' ministry contexts, and selected readings and study. Participants form lasting relationships with one another as they explore complex challenges in a supportive and collegial environment.

**Faith+Lead Practices** is a collection of action learning experiments that you can try in your ministry context. Get step-by-step guidance on how to lead Dwelling in the Word, discern God's presence from a lawn chair, listen to spiritual stories from people outside your congregation, create a neighborhood prayer station, and much more.

**Faith+Lead's Seeds Project** provides a cohort with a yearlong fellowship that combines learning in community along with opportunities for professional development for ministry entrepreneurs starting new things. The program is intended for innovative leaders who are passionate about the gospel, eager to grow, and creative in their approach to developing new ways of being the church and cultivating Christian faith in a changing world.

faith+lead
LUTHER SEMINARY

# Notes

## Introduction: Defining Faithful Innovation

1  The stories that open each chapter are fictional representations of what we have heard from real leaders.

2  The language of "longings and losses" comes from Scott Cormode, *The Innovative Church* (Grand Rapids, MI: Baker Academic, 2020), 9.

3  See Alan J. Roxburgh, *Joining God, Remaking Church, Changing the World* (New York: Morehouse, 2015), ix.

4  Roxburgh, ix.

5  Peter J. Denning and Robert Dunham, *The Innovator's Way* (Cambridge, MA: MIT Press, 2010), 6.

6  Cormode, *Innovative Church*, 3.

7  Peter G. Nordhouse, *Leadership: Theory and Practice*, 5th ed. (Los Angeles: Sage, 2010), 3.

8  Scott Cormode, "Multi-layered Leadership: The Christian Leader as Builder, Shepherd, Gardener," *Journal of Religious Leadership* 1, no. 2 (Fall 2002): 71.

## Chapter One: Why Lydia Doesn't Go to Your Church

1  Gregory A. Smith, "About Three-in-Ten US Adults Are Now Religiously Unaffiliated," Pew Research Center, December 14, 2021, https://www.pewresearch.org/religion/2021/12/14/about-three-in-ten-u-s-adults-are-now-religiously-unaffiliated/.

2   "Why Americans Go (and Don't Go) to Religious Services," Pew Research Center, August 1, 2018, https://www.pewresearch.org/religion/2018/08/01/why-americans-go-to-religious-services/.

3   Ted Smith, "No Longer Shall They Teach One Another: The End of Theological Education" (Virtual Sprunt Lecture Series, Union Presbyterian Seminary, May 3–5, 2021). Charles Taylor refers to this as the Age of Mobilization. See A Secular Age (Cambridge, MA: Belknap, 2007), 423–72.

4   Taylor, Secular Age, 473–504.

5   The term inherited church describes existing congregations and church systems. They carry the treasures of the inheritance of Christian faith through the generations, even as they may need to adapt to connect with today's neighbors.

6   See Taylor, Secular Age, 11.

7   See Andrew Root, Faith Formation in a Secular Age (Grand Rapids, MI: Baker Academic, 2017), 113–14.

8   See Hartmut Rosa, Alienation and Acceleration (Malmøgade, Denmark: NSU Press, 2013).

9   Anne Case and Angus Deaton, Deaths of Despair and the Future of Capitalism (Princeton, NJ: Princeton University Press, 2021).

10  See Michael Dimok and Richard Wike, "America Is Exceptional in the Nature of Its Political Divide," Pew Research Center, November 13, 2020, https://www.pewresearch.org/fact-tank/2020/11/13/america-is-exceptional-in-the-nature-of-its-political-divide/.

## Chapter Two: Listen

1   This Listen-Act-Share process builds on similar processes created by some of our mentors and colleagues, to whom we are grateful: Alan Roxburgh, Craig Van Gelder, Fiona Watts, Patrick Keifert, Mark Lau Branson, and others.

2   Cormode, Innovative Church, 39.

3    This version of Dwelling in the Word is a variation on a practice devel-
      oped by Church Innovations Institute. See www.churchinnovations
      .org/dwelling-in-the-word.

4    See Mark Lau Branson and Juan Martinez, *Churches, Cultures, and
      Leadership* (Downers Grove, IL: InterVarsity, 2011), 55–56. See
      also Scott Cormode, *Making Spiritual Sense* (Nashville: Abingdon,
      2006).

5    Craig Van Gelder and Dwight Zscheile, *The Missional Church in Per-
      spective* (Grand Rapids, MI: Baker Academic, 2011), 5.

## Chapter Three: Act

1    For more on the difference between technical and adaptive chal-
      lenges, see Ronald Heifetz and Marty Linsky, *Leadership on the Line*
      (Boston: Harvard Business Review Press, 2017), 14.

## Chapter Four: Share

1    Ben Witherington, "Lydia (Person)," in *The Anchor Yale Bible Dictio-
      nary: K–N*, ed. David Noel Freedman (New Haven, CT: Yale Univer-
      sity Press, 1992), 422.

2    See, for instance, Elizabeth Drescher, *Choosing Our Religion: The
      Spiritual Lives of America's Nones* (New York: Oxford University Press,
      2016).

3    See Everett M. Rogers, *Diffusion of Innovations*, 5th ed. (New York:
      Free Press, 2003), 360.

## Chapter Five: Faithful Innovation as
## a Way of Life for the Church

1    For more on the difference between technical and adaptive chal-
      lenges, see Heifetz and Linsky, *Leadership on the Line*, 14.

2   See SmarterEveryDay, "The Backwards Brain Bicycle—Smarter Every Day 133," April 24, 2015, YouTube video, 7:57, https://youtu.be/MFzDaBzBILO, to learn more about the backwards bicycle.

3   See the websites of Fresh Expressions UK (https://freshexpressions .org.uk), Fresh Expressions US (https://freshexpressions.com), or Archbishop's Council on Mission and Public Affairs, *Mission Shaped Church: Church Planting and Fresh Expressions of Church in a Changing Context* (London: Church House, 2004).

4   This insight was shared by Church of England Fresh Expressions leaders Bishop Mike Harrison, Heather Cracknell, Ed Olsworth-Peter, and Nick Shepherd in a personal conversation with Dwight Zscheile in December 2019.

## Chapter Six: Faithful Innovation as a Way of Leading

1   Cormode, *Innovative Church*, 9.

2   See Ps 79 or Ps 85 for examples of lament psalms.

3   Peter Scazzero, *Emotionally Healthy Spirituality* (Grand Rapids, MI: Zondervan, 2006), 31.

4   Scazzero, 31.

5   This is a simplified version of a practice that originated in Ignatian spirituality.

6   Heifetz and Linsky, *Leadership on the Line*, 142.

7   Scazzero, *Emotionally Healthy Spirituality*, 34.

8   Scazzero, 56–58.

9   Ruth Haley Barton, *Sacred Rhythms* (Downers Grove, IL: InterVarsity, 2006), 137.

10  Rob Muthiah, *The Sabbath Experiment: Spiritual Formation for Living in a Non-stop World* (Eugene, OR: Cascade, 2015), 19.

11  Muthiah, 23.

12  The APEST Personal Vocational Assessment was developed by Alan Hirsch. See the 5Q Collective website (https://5qcentral.com/product/apest-vocational-assessment) to learn more about the assessment.